3/13

The Teach Yourself series has been trusted around the world for
over sixty years. This new series of 'In A Week' business books
is designed to help people at all levels and around the world to
further their careers. Learn in a week, what the experts learn in

Christine Harvey is an award winning speaker, and has addressed two parliaments plus audiences of 2,500. She's founder of Effective Presentation Seminars and Successful Selling Seminars taught to thousands in Europe, America and Asia, including corporations and the US Military. She has authored seven books published in 28 languages, including *In Pursuit of Profit, Secrets of the World's Top Sales Performers, Can a Girl Run for President?, Successful Selling In A Week, Successful People Skills In A Week*, and *Successful Personal Impact In A Week*. Her writing success plus expertise in self-presentation, makes this a must-have book for anyone who wants to impact decision making and catapult their career.

Personal Impact

Christine Harvey

www.inaweek.co.uk

First published in Great Britain in 2013 by Hodder & Stoughton. An Hachette UK company.

First published in US in 2013 by The McGraw-Hill Companies, Inc.

This edition published 2013

British Library Cataloguing in Publication Data: a catalogue record for this title is available from the British Library.

Library of Congress Catalog Card Number: on file.

10 9 8 7 6 5 4 3 2 1

Typeset by Cenveo Publisher Services.

Printed in Great Britain by CPI Cox & Wyman, Reading.

Hodder & Stoughton policy is to use papers that are natural, renewable and recyclable products and made from wood grown in sustainable forests. The logging and manufacturing processes are expected to conform to the environmental regulations of the country of origin.

Hodder & Stoughton Ltd

338 Euston Road

London NW1 3BH

www.hodder.co.uk.

Contents

Introduction

When I was 21, I noticed that people who moved ahead the fastest in their careers were not necessarily the ones with the best education, contrary to my belief about success. Indeed not! Instead they were the ones who could put their ideas across most effectively. They were people who were not afraid to speak out at meetings, or even go up to a microphone.

This made me think. All the years of education are necessary. Yes. But there is more to getting ahead in life. I became a fervent student of the power of persuasion. What was it? What were the component parts?

I realized I had a long way to go. At my first professional job, I was afraid to even speak on the phone. Later I discovered that anything we throw ourselves into, we can achieve with practice. Soon I not only conquered the fear of the phone, but I bit the bullet and signed up for a course in public speaking! Again I discovered that pushing the edge of the comfort zone allowed me to achieve the unthinkable. In addition to raising my family, I started my own company – a huge risk and challenge. I had to learn to sell, and to motive people. I felt both were essential to success. Soon I had customers in Europe and America, and later in Asia.

But in the back of my mind was always this concept of education vs. personal projection. Why were the best-educated people not necessarily the ones making it to the top? The answer was clear. They hadn't learned the skills of personal projection, personal impact. They hadn't learned the importance of motivation, or how to do it.

I continued on with my business, and was later elected Chair of a London Chamber of Commerce – the first woman and first American to hold that position. I also decided I wanted to become a world class motivational speaker. I wasn't sure how I would measure that, but speaking before groups of 2500, at the likes of IBM, helped me to realize that goal. I always aimed to leave lasting impressions – ones that helped each and every person to realize their own inner potential. After all, if a gal who was once afraid of speaking on the phone can gain the competence and courage to address not one, but two parliaments, then surely anyone can do it. With the right information and the determination not to give up, I believed that anyone could achieve their highest potential.

Last week a gratifying article hit the internet. Some 15 years after addressing managers of the Sony Corporation, I received this blog posting from their former Managing Director in the UK, David Pearson. *'Christine Harvey is a brilliant motivational speaker. She advised our managers to blow the whistle on good behaviour, instead of bad. After her speech, I ordered whistles for everyone. The sound of whistles went on for days, reminding everyone of their new management effectiveness!'*

I believe my message stuck. And I believe it will for you too when you apply the principles I've laid out here. It's not about presentations – although this is critical. It's about you. It's about your inner potential. It's about how you put yourself across. Whether you find yourself in a job interview, or asking for a promotion, or trying to convince anyone of anything, these skills are mandatory for success. If it happened for me, as well as the thousands I've trained on three continents, it can happen for you.

In today's world, with the competition for jobs, promotions and customers, *plus* the visibility we have on Facebook, YouTube and social media, we need to take charge of our personal impact – it's essential to our success.

Please write to me and let me know your successes – ChristineHarvey@ChristineHarvey.com or via the publishers.

Wishing you every success and joy,

Christine Harvey

SUNDAY

Conquer non-verbal power

Whether you are giving your first presentation tomorrow, or you're a veteran speaker, it's essential for you to know that your non-verbal actions have tremendous power. It would be foolhardy to ignore this aspect of your impact.

Think about the presenters on television, on YouTube, people in politics and those at work. Think of people who win their point, time after time. Is it their actual words that win the point? Or... is it the way they use their voice to say their words? Or... is it the way they use their body to say the words, for example, their facial expression, the position of their body as they sit or stand, or perhaps the energy they exude?

In this chapter, you'll leave nothing to chance. You'll leave no room for embarrassment or lessening of your personal impact. To the contrary, this chapter shows you the importance of your *non-verbal impact* including:

The power of eye contact

The power stance

Walking with purpose

Magnifying your energy to vanquish fear

Using gestures for high impact

Projection of conviction

Three aspects of impact

Whether in a meeting at work, or on the stage for a presentation, certain things are critical to getting your point across and achieving success in your career. These include how you walk, how you move your hands, how you use your voice, even your eye contact – *all* are important!

The fact is that human beings process information through a number of senses. They are impacted with the tone, sincerity and conviction of our voice. We project varying degrees of credibility by the way we move, the way we hold ourselves, the energy we project, the conviction in our eyes, our face, our body.

Let's break down personal impact into these three categories:

1 Your words
2 Your voice
3 Your non-verbal movements and actions

What percentage impact do you think each category has on our listeners? There has been much research and much controversy among experts of the exact percentages to be attributed to each of the three categories. One of the most widely accepted findings are these. See if it surprises you. Three aspects of impact: Words 7%, Voice 38%, Non-Verbal Actions 55% = 100%.

Is it different from what you expected? Of course we need words to express our thoughts. At school we learn to put emphasis on words with little or no emphasis on the remainder of our personal impact.

So let's look at what makes up our non-verbal impact.

Five aspects of non-verbal impact

Eye contact

Stance

Walking

Gestures of arms, hands and face

Projection of conviction

The material ahead will contribute enormously to your authority, confidence, and leadership. You'll be surprised at its impact the moment you use it.

Power of eye contact

Eye contact is the king of non-verbals. In a recent rating of live audiences, presenters who had no eye contact with the audience were rated 40% less effective than those who had eye contact. Whether you want to make an impact in meetings, one to one, or to crowds of thousands, eye contacts is all important. When I train trainers and presenters, it's first on my list. Without good eye contact, your sincerity and impact is lost.

Since you don't have an audience as you're reading this book, you'll need to practise through visualization. Perhaps you've heard about the highly successful experiment with ball players. They used visualization *without* the ball to dramatically short cut their learning curve. Subconsciously, before we do anything in life, we see ourselves doing it. What you'll do here is to speed up the process, consciously.

Perfecting 'eye contact' impact

Do this powerful practice now. Imagine you're in a group meeting at work. Your colleagues are around the same table. Imagine looking directly into the eyes of each person as you speak. See the person across from you. Then look left at the person next to you and do the same. See your boss at the head of the table and do the same.

Now see yourself making a presentation to 20, using the same great eye contact. Now to 40. Now 100. Keep going, letting the group get larger and larger, using the same powerful eye contact.

How does it feel? Does it feel ridiculous, awkward or inhibiting? If so, repeat the process. With six practices in total, you will feel like an expert. Then practise it tonight at dinner, or at lunch with your colleagues or family, as you talk about anything. *You shouldn't wait to give a presentation to practise good eye contact. Develop your skill now and remember to use it daily until it becomes a habit.*

Don't draw the wrong attention – use the power stance

Imagine, for a moment, an absent-minded professor pacing in front of his class. Conjure up a picture of him walking with a slight slouch, hands behind his back, pacing back and forth at the front of the classroom as he speaks, looking at the ceiling and floor. What do his students absorb? Do they hear his words or are they distracted by his movement?

Let's take a tip from television producers. They know that 'the eye of the viewer is greedier than the ear'. As humans we are more easily attracted by what we see than what we hear.

TIP

Perfecting 'power stance' impact
Imagine giving a presentation, using great eye contact as in the last section. This time stand up, and keep your feet planted firmly on the floor.

- *Centre your weight evenly over both feet.*
- *Feel the power of your stance.*
- *Keep yourself 'planted' as you imagine speaking.*
- *Experience your power with this stance thus not distracting your audience from your message.*

How does it feel? Are you ready to build upon it? Let's take it further and study the impact of walking with purpose.

Walk with purpose

Do you think it would be good for a presenter to stand planted to one spot for their whole presentation? No, it provides no interest or variety. Should we pace like absent-minded professors then? No, that distracts our audience. What then?

The answer is to walk with purpose. Just as you choose your words, you'll choose your actions. What could those actions be? It depends on what kind of impact you want to create.

What if you want to create rapport with the audience, for example? You might walk up to someone in the first or second row, lean forward and say something while lowering your voice. What about a surprise element? You could walk to a table or podium and pound it with your fist just as you deliver an important line. They'll never forget it. Or perhaps you'll move to a flip chart or a screen. If so, walk with a sense of purpose, even a sense of urgency. Then your listeners will feel the importance of your message. Conversely, if you were to saunter across, you would give the non-verbal message of unimportance.

Remember that your non-verbal projection could account for as much as 55% of your impact. You've spent a lot of time preparing your subject – perhaps years of study and experience. We don't want you to negate your expertise now, through ineffective delivery.

Magnify your energy to vanquish fear

'You will always have butterflies before a presentation. Just make sure you keep them flying in formation.' That's the advice of Dale Carnegie, the legendary founder of Effective Speaking and Human Relations, a course delivered to millions all over the world. Simply think of the butterflies as valuable energy available to you that you can focus on your audience, your delivery and your message.

When you use energy, you radiate life. People feel your energy and are energized by it. They are drawn to you and to your message. Energy is not a perishable commodity. In fact, energy dissipates when not in use. Energy is rechargeable. The more you use, the more you get.

Have you heard the story about the petite woman who lifted a car off her son after an accident? She saved his life. The event triggered her adrenaline flow which gave her enormous power. Was that adrenaline always there ready to be on called upon? Yes, it was. Otherwise it could not be released in an instant.

We have the same power. Athletes release it for athletic events. You can release it for presentations or anytime you need it.

The secret of energy is one of the most misunderstood subjects of human nature. I often have audience members come up to me and say, 'Mrs Harvey, I really admire your energy.' What they don't know is that one hour before my talk, I may have felt completely unenergetic. Just as athletes get mentally prepared on the way to a match, we can do the same. Here's what I do. On the way to my presentation, I start to let my enthusiasm build. This lets the adrenaline flow and the energy follows.

Now let's master the next aspect of projecting your authority.

Using gestures for impact

Let's consider any movement of the body to be a gesture. Hands, arms, legs, face. Think of the face alone. What you do with your face, combined with the feeling behind your message, has more to do with conviction than anything else you can do.

Facial gestures

Many new presenters are surprised by this. They don't realize *what* their face does because it is so automatic. They don't realize they can control it or change it.

The best way to inspire change is by watching yourself on video. I studied television interviewing techniques with many BBC radio presenters who were moving into television. Most were shocked by seeing their facial features for the first time on the screen, and this shock provoked change.

Before that training, people often came up to me after my speeches and told me that I reminded them of Margaret Thatcher. After I saw myself on the television monitor, I discovered why – my facial gestures were so serious and emphatic. I could be talking about an issue as simple as cats having kittens and make it seem as grave as a 200% increase in the national deficit. After the training I didn't lose my ability to do that, but I immediately learned to be more selective in its use.

The point is this. When you know what you are doing, you can change it. If you don't have a video camera, sit in front of a large mirror while you talk on the phone. What you'll discover will be invaluable to you. However, if you are going to take your career seriously, you must see yourself on video. You'll notice some habits that you'll want to change. Everyone else sees them. Don't let yourself be the last to know!

Facial signals

You can also use your facial expressions to signal what's to come. You can be very serious before an emotional line. You can even pause and contemplate. Or you can smile or laugh before a humorous line.

Let your face be congruent with your message and let your facial expression precede your words!

Why would you bother to even think about this? If you watch television with the sound off, you'll see how important it is. As we said before, human beings take in information through all their senses. Their eyes take in your facial expressions and powerful messages about your intention, your sincerity, and your conviction.

Perfecting 'facial gesture' impact

Stop and think for a moment. What is it that triggers the face to do what it does? The main aspect is feeling.

1 Think of an issue you feel strongly about, then pick one sentence to describe it. For example, it could be, 'Our school system needs to be improved.' What feeling do you have? Is it a feeling of concern? A feeling of anger or rage or excitement? Let it show.
2 Look in the mirror and say the sentence three times.
3 First say it with no feeling.
4 Then say it with mild feeling.
5 Lastly say it with strong feeling and conviction – as if your life or your child's life depended on it.

Impact Journal

What did you see in the three versions – no feeling, mild feeling, and strong feeling? Create an Impact Journal and jot down the difference in your facial expressions. Keeping the journal this week will allow you to review important points in the future to heighten your personal impact, before an important presentation or meeting.

Gestures of your arms and hands

We all use our hands and arms unconsciously when talking one to one, or in a group. The negative ways include fidgeting with your tie, necklace or ring, or jingling the keys or money in your pocket. Now it's time to consciously harness the power of gestures for positive impact.

Here's a rule of thumb. Simply magnify your gestures by the size of the group. Consider this. If you spoke to a group of 200 people using the same gestures as you would speaking to one person across a dinner table, the gestures would be practically unnoticeable. If you magnify your gestures to fit a group of 200 and use those gestures when you speak to one person, it looks equally absurd.

Here's how to magnify your gestures. Think of your arm first. It has three joints – the wrist, the elbow, the shoulder. Small gestures come from wrist movement, medium gestures come from elbow movement, large gestures come from shoulder movement. If you speak to any group larger than ten people, you should be using shoulder movements. Try it in the mirror and you'll see the difference in impact.

Perfecting 'arm and hand gesture' impact

Sit or stand where you are now. Say the same sentence you said earlier with feeling, such as 'Our school system needs to be improved.' Any sentence will do.

1 Say it once while moving your hand at the wrist.
2 Say it again moving your arm at the elbow.

---

3 Do it again moving your arm from the shoulder with a large emphatic movement.

Repeat the cycle until you've done each six times – small gesture, medium gesture, large gesture. After six times you will feel quite at ease with each.

Gestures to avoid

Most neophyte presenters do very well with gestures. It's simply a matter of being yourself, and using your hands in a more magnified way than you would when speaking to a friend.

However, some people want to be further forewarned about what not to do.

List of Don'ts

1 Don't distract your audience from your message with unnecessary non-verbal movements.
2 Don't let yourself indulge in jangling the keys or money in your pocket, twisting your tie or jewellery, or touching your glasses incessantly.
3 Don't stroll without purpose – this brings attention to you physically rather than to your message.
4 Don't fiddle with your hands – instead use them for conscious gesturing, as in showing the size of something, or the direction of something, or let them be still.

Now reflect on your progress. You've delved into one of the most powerful aspects of speaking, yet something we never study at school: your non-verbal impact. You've studied eye contact, power stance, walking with purpose, magnifying your energy and making an impact with gestures.

What creates projection of conviction?

Think about what causes the projection of conviction. There are three components:

1 The face, driven by feeling, as discussed above
2 Energy as discussed above
3 Emphasis of voice

When people speak with conviction, they are taken more seriously. If you want to speak with more conviction, be it to your peers or to an audience, apply the three principles above every day. You can use projection of conviction at the supermarket talking to the check-out staff, or at the bank, or at work. You'll be amazed at the difference in seriousness with which people receive you. When you learn to use it every day, you can draw upon it more easily in presentations of any kind.

Impact Journal
1 *Watch different presenters on television or YouTube. You'll see major differences in the way people project themselves.*
2 *Now think of the people you know of high credibility and impact who always win their points. What common thread do you see?*
3 *List what you notice in your impact journal. Keep this journal with you and record what you see in others that is effective over the next seven days. Watch face, hands, body angle, stance, movement, energy, eye contact. Note what you think is effective and ineffective. This will allow you to easily incorporate effective non-verbal actions into your own personal impact.*

Social media application

Direct eye contact with the camera is powerful and engaging, both in still and moving images. Whether on video, such as television and YouTube, or with still images such as Facebook, be sure to apply the eye contact principles.

With video, applied to all social media, the power stance will give you more credibility than bouncing around while standing or sitting. With video shots above the waist, be sure to magnify your energy through enthusiasm and emphasis in your voice plus facial expressions. Refer to the section on 'what creates projection of conviction'.

Remember too, the power of gestures. Using your hands and arm gestures creates impact. Take a moment to watch TV *without* the sound and you will pick up some great tips. Then adjust it to your personality for the effective use of non-verbals.

Although social media is meant to be quick and easy, often with a philosophy of 'just get it out there' and 'don't worry about perfection', we all know that human beings judge what we see and hear. Keep this in mind and let your personality come through naturally as you employ the methods above.

Most importantly, dare to utilize what you've learned in this chapter. For knowledge without action will lead nowhere!

Summary

Today you learned about non-verbal actions that could account for up to 55% of your impact. These include eye contact, power stance, walking with purpose, magnifying energy to vanquish fear and using gestures for impact.

Research has shown that audiences give speakers a 40% less effectiveness rating when there is no eye contact. On the positive side, good eye contact, whether one to one, on television, YouTube or with audiences, makes more impact than any other non-verbal action.

You also learned that the 'absent-minded professor' habit of pacing back and forth causes distraction from our message. By using both the power stance, and walking with purpose, we dramatically heighten our impact.

Fear, you learned, is a form of energy that can be harnessed for positive impact. We all have a feeling of butterflies before a presentation but, by keeping the butterflies flying in formation, we transform the energy to our benefit.

Gestures of the face, hands and arms, are so automatic that we rarely think of them or of their impact, either as positive or negative. Yet, by knowing and practising the rules you've learned, you can eliminate the negative and greatly enhance the positive personal impact.

SUNDAY

MONDAY

TUESDAY

WEDNESDAY

THURSDAY

FRIDAY

SATURDAY

Fact-check (answers at the back)

1. What percentage of your impact is said to be based on non-verbal actions?
   a) 5% ☐
   b) 25% ☐
   c) 45% ☐
   d) 55% ☐

2. In ratings from live audience, the speakers received what percentage less effectiveness rating when there was no eye contact?
   a) 10% ☐
   b) 20% ☐
   c) 40% ☐
   d) 80% ☐

3. According to research done for television producers, what human sense creates the most impact for viewers?
   a) Hearing ☐
   b) Seeing ☐
   c) Feeling ☐
   d) Smelling ☐

4. Aimless pacing has proven to be a distraction from our message. Instead we should
   a) walk with purpose ☐
   b) take a power stance ☐
   c) both of the above ☐
   d) none of the above ☐

5. A legendary trainer of public speaking advised his students not to fear the feeling of butterflies before a presentation. Instead he advised them to
   a) keep them flying in formation ☐
   b) take a break before the presentation ☐
   c) take a stiff drink ☐
   d) cancel the engagement ☐

6. Which of the following is true about energy?
   a) It's not a perishable commodity ☐
   b) It dissipates when not in use ☐
   c) It's rechargeable ☐
   d) All of the above ☐

7. The best way to force change in your unconscious non-verbal actions is to
   a) look in the mirror when you talk on the telephone ☐
   b) watch yourself on video ☐
   c) scold yourself ☐
   d) ask a friend ☐

8. Which following non-verbal habits diminish your personal impact and should be changed?
   a) Walking with your hands clenched behind your back ☐
   b) Fidgeting with your necklace, tie, or ring ☐
   c) Jiggling the keys or money in your pocket ☐
   d) All of the above ☐

9. What causes us to project conviction?
a) Our face, driven by feeling ☐
b) Energy ☐
c) Emphasis of voice ☐
d) All of the above ☐

...tures with our ..., the bigger the group, ...er the gestures need to be. You should be using arm movements originating from the shoulder for groups larger than
a) 10 ☐
b) 20 ☐
c) 40 ☐
d) 80 ☐

MONDAY

Avoid embarrassment and discrediting yourself

Have you ever heard anyone preface their statement like this? *'I don't know if this is important or not but ...'* It happens in meetings and in personal conversations every day.

What does that preface do? It sets up doubt in the listener's mind immediately. It's like a siren shouting: 'Not important, not important.' When this happens, both the statement *and* the speaker lose credibility.

In this chapter we'll look at how to compose your message for high impact and credibility. You'll also look at your personal experiences and rediscover the wealth of knowledge and strengths you can draw upon. This knowledge is essential to bringing credibility to yourself and to the points you're making. Without this, your listeners have no incentive to listen or take action. And without this, you have no personal impact.

We'll look at three keys for making your message powerful, even *before* you divulge your message. These include personal credibility, expert credibility, and reputable source credibility.

Also in this chapter you'll learn:

How to avoid discrediting yourself

How to create credibility prefaces

How to draw upon your life experience and strengths for any subject

Create credibility prefaces

Many people discredit themselves unintentionally. If you do, stop immediately. It is a pity to have good ideas lost and ignored simply because of a discrediting habit.

Listen to yourself speak. Do you have other discrediting habits? Some people say, 'This may not be relevant but ...' Others say, 'I'm not an expert but ...' Or, 'Like John said...' All of these discredit you or your message. After all, why should they listen after you tell them it's not relevant, or that you are not an expert, or that they already heard it from John? Their brain then shuts your message out.

Here's a powerful way to change it. Use a credibility preface to tell the listeners why they should believe in your message. Try this at your next meeting or presentation and see the difference.

Your preface can take one of these three forms:

1 Personal Credibility
Example: *'When I was chairman of the London Chamber of Commerce I discovered ...'* (make your point)

2 Expert Credibility
Example: *'Susan Jones, founder of one of the largest direct sales organizations in the world believes ...'* (make your point)

3 Reputable Source Credibility
Example: *'The Wall Street Journal stated in its January 22nd issue that ...'* (make your point)

Are you ready to try it? Good. Jump in. You'll see it's easier than you think.

Perfecting 'Personal Credibility Prefaces'

Think of any point you could make.

Now create your Personal Credibility Preface. It might sound like this. *'Over the eight years that I've been in this business, in three successful companies,* (that's your Personal Credibility Preface, now give your point, such as ...) *I've observed that the people who move ahead the fastest are the ones who have good people skills.'*

Combine your own preface and point and see how it sounds.

Don't confuse this with boasting about yourself. You are simply giving your point the credibility it needs to be taken seriously. Look at it this way. If you didn't want your message taken seriously, you wouldn't bother to say it. So why not give it the emphasis it deserves? Your ideas deserve to be taken seriously. When only a few people speak out with credibility, the world makes decisions based upon too few people. Today I hope that you are going to change that balance by using credibility prefaces.

Perfecting 'Expert Credibility Prefaces'

Think of another point you could make.

Now create your Expert Credibility Preface. For example, *'Mike Smith, our new CEO* (that's your Expert Credibility Preface, now give your point, such as ...) *says that the people who move ahead the fastest are the ones who have developed good people skills.'*

Combine your own preface and point and see how it sounds.

Perfecting 'Reputable Source Prefaces'

Think of another point you could make.

Now create your Reputable Source Preface such as *'A BBC documentary on careers* (that's your Reputable Source Preface, now give your point, such as ...) *showed that the people who move ahead the fastest are the ones who display good skills working with people.'*

Combine your own preface and point and see how it sounds.

SUNDAY · MONDAY · TUESDAY · WEDNESDAY · THURSDAY · FRIDAY · SATURDAY

Well done. By using credibility prefaces before your statement, you are giving your listeners proof that your statement has widespread validity and is worth listening to.

Now let's look at your lifetime of strengths to add more power to your communication.

Draw upon your strengths to discuss any topic

Do you think you could talk for six hours straight on a string of subjects pulled from a hat? I didn't think I could, until I participated in a charity Talkathon in London. It made me realize that we all have a repertoire of experience that lies dormant in our minds until we are called upon to use it.

Why is this important? The answer is this. The greater your confidence in your repertoire of experience, the stronger your response will be when called upon in an impromptu situation, be it in front of the boss, in a meeting or in a formal presentation. Or even when asking for an increase in pay, or handling a job interview!

Although this is the longest exercise in the book, the results you gain from it will be enormous. You'll be referring back to this section for sources of credibility, for proving your point, for incidents with high impact and even for humour. So dig in and enjoy. You'll be amazed at the wealth of experience and strengths you bring to every situation.

Strengths from types of organizations

In the exercises below, you'll discover the huge diversity of knowledge that you bring to any situation. By referring to these personal experiences, you give yourself high credibility and make your comments interesting and memorable.

In your impact journal, list every 'type' of company you have ever worked for – paid or unpaid, part time or full time. Go back to your earliest job. See example below.

-
-
-
-
-
-

- For example, mine looks like this:
- Computer Company
- Own Company – Property
- Own Company – Training
- Educational Institute
- Radio
- TV
- Publishing

List yours.

You are already getting a sense of the breadth of your experience.

Strengths from types of functions

Now list every function you had in any company or organization. For example, sales, administrator, finance, reporter, etc.

-
-
-
-
-

List everything you did, even if it was for a short time, or even volunteer work.

Strengths from recognition

Now list any awards or special recognition you gained in business,
professional organizations, sports, hobby, music or school, even
those not related to your career. Go back to early childhood, and
come up to the current day.

- •
- •
- •
- •
- •

- •
- •
- •
- •
- •

Good. It's important to acknowledge yourself and see the lists of
knowledge, strengths and experience growing.

Strengths from competence, interests and enjoyment

List your areas of competence. Include things at home, and in the
community. For example: repair the car, wallpaper a room, keep
people working as a team, etc.

Include all your interest areas, the subjects you have studied or
enjoyed – school, seminars, books, lectures, sports hobbies, and
activities.

Also list things you simply like to do, or volunteer to do – walk
in the woods, be with family, do gardening, help at child's school,
service organizations.

And anything else you excel in – teaching people, motivating
people, creative, artistic, etc.

- •
- •
- •
- •
- •
- •
- •
- •
- •

- •
- •
- •
- •
- •
- •
- •
- •
- •

Reflect on the wealth of subject areas you have to draw upon to discuss any topic from your entries above.

Impact Journal
1 **Pick any subject you might need or like to speak about.**
2 **From your lists above, choose three of your strengths or experiences that could link to it as a Personal Credibility Preface.**
3 **Record these in your impact journal.**

Perhaps you've heard it said that most people are more afraid of speaking in public than of dying. This won't happen if you concentrate on your strengths and background knowledge above. Instead you'll realize the wealth of experience, knowledge, interests and expertise that lies within you, ready to be called in to action. Keep these lists to refer to in the future.

Social media application

Let's consider your credibility first with regard to social media. Even with Twitter, a few words are enough to put across your credibility, along with a link to your message. For example, 'Find out what I discovered when I chaired the XYZ function', will draw more attention than not mentioning your position. The same is true with Facebook, LinkedIn, YouTube, etc.

Experiment with different ways of putting across your credibility and see which works best according to your field, but don't neglect it. When you find the best method, use it to your advantage.

Next, draw upon your background experiences to connect with people. Others will always be drawn to you by similar experiences. For example, if you want to connect with a certain author but you have no knowledge of their field, look to see what other interests they have that are compatible with yours, and connect through that. And if you have credibility in that compatible interest area, use that too.

SUNDAY
MONDAY
TUESDAY
WEDNESDAY
THURSDAY
FRIDAY
SATURDAY

Summary

In this chapter, you learned three key ways to give credibility to your points. You saw that before you make an important statement, you can preface it with a credibility point about yourself, or you can attribute it to an expert, or you can quote the source from which the point comes.

All of these prefaces make your listener take notice. They also prevent you from discrediting yourself. All of these bring credibility to you and heighten your image and impact.

Another important aspect of this chapter is learning to draw upon your strengths from the diversity of your background. Whether you are asking for an increase in pay, a promotion, or you are addressing a group about a subject close to your heart, the ability to quickly draw upon your strengths will bring you success and heighten your personal impact.

If you were tempted to skip writing the exercises, I urge you to go back and fill in the pages or your journal. Seeing your experiences in writing is a huge confidence builder, and will serve you surprisingly well in the future. Its impact is much greater in writing than seeing it in the mind's eye.

SUNDAY
MONDAY
TUESDAY
WEDNESDAY
THURSDAY
FRIDAY
SATURDAY

Fact-check (answers at the back)

1. When someone starts their sentence with a preface such as, 'I don't know if this is important, but...' the listeners think what?
   a) He/she is modest and I like them ❑
   b) It sets up doubt and lessens credibility ❑
   c) It seems friendly ❑
   d) It's a nice way to start ❑

2. There are three types of credibility prefaces that can enhance your image and your message. Choose the one below which is NOT a credibility preface.
   a) Personal credibility ❑
   b) Expert credibility ❑
   c) Reputable source credibility ❑
   d) Controversial credibility ❑

3. An example of personal credibility is
   a) When I was captain of the ABC Rowing Club ... ❑
   b) During my 10 years in the manufacturing industry ... ❑
   c) When I won the award for sales ... ❑
   d) All of the above ❑

4. Using personal credibility prefaces should not be confused with boasting about oneself. Which of the following are true with regard to credibility prefaces?
   a) People will take you more seriously ❑
   b) People will take your message more seriously ❑
   c) Your ideas deserve to be taken seriously ❑
   d) All of the above ❑

5. When you use an expert credibility preface, it could sound like this:
   a) Mike Smith, our CEO, says... ❑
   b) The successful chairperson of XYZ Company doesn't use this method, and neither should we ... ❑
   c) Susan Jones, founder of the ABC Foundation, has had great success with the method I am going to show you now ... ❑
   d) All of the above ❑

6. A reputable source preface could sound like this:
   a) The BBC special pointed out ... ❑
   b) The *Wall St Journal* quoted ... ❑
   c) The best-selling book, *XYZ*, said ... ❑
   d) All of the above ❑

7. When using either the expert or the reputable source preface, you are basically telling people
a) that you have widespread proof that your statement is valid and should be taken seriously ☐
b) that you have influence ☐
c) that you are intelligent ☐
d) all the above ☐

8. Listing points about your background will help you to
a) ask for a promotion ☐
b) address a group of thousands ☐
c) answer an impromptu question quickly and effectively ☐
d) all of the above ☐

9. Seeing the list of your background points in writing is more effective than
a) seeing it in your mind's eye ☐
b) telling your friends ☐
c) not doing it ☐
d) all of the above ☐

10. By making a list of your background points in the exercises above, which of the following is NOT true?
a) You'll be surprised at the diversity of your knowledge ☐
b) You'll spend time and find it useless in the end ☐
c) You'll discover things about yourself that you have long forgotten ☐
d) You'll see yourself in a new light, and discover the credibility you have to talk on numerous subjects ☐

TUESDAY

Structure your presentation to prove your point masterfully

Now we arrive at the exciting moment of our personal impact – what to say and how to say it! We can take a lesson from screenplay writers who make every scene and every line of dialogue count. There are no extraneous lines and no extraneous scenes. Everything is there for a reason. Everything leads to the final plot point and everything proves the point the writer is trying to make.

In presentations or in delivering any message, even one to one, it's the same. You have to know your message, like the plot of the movie. Then each point and connected proof must lead to and support the message. When you've set up your presentation like this, your audience will be left with a powerful message, for it will have moved them in some way.

In this important chapter you will learn how to prove your points masterfully by:

Structuring your presentation for high impact

Using the power of proof

Developing logical and emotional proof

Using numbers and statistics for power

Using references for persuasion

Using expert quotes for credibility

Making your point stick

Making smooth transitions

Logical and emotional proof

Getting our point across would be easy if everyone believed what we wanted to say without proof. But they don't. If you listen to a 10-year-old child, their conversation often sounds like this. 'My father is so strong, he can lift a car,' one child says. The other responds, 'Oh yeah, prove it.'

People never change. They like to have proof with everything they hear, but it doesn't stop there. There is not one, but *two* types of proof you need to provide. One is logical proof and other is what we'll call emotional proof, the intangible focusing on human needs.

With regards to emotional proof, perhaps Albert Einstein put it best when he said, 'I did not arrive at my understanding of the fundamental laws of the universe through my rational mind.'

Presenting our ideas effectively, whether to a group or one to one, is much like selling a concept. Most people start out thinking that all decisions are based upon logical needs.

On the logical level, the manager wants to buy machinery in order to increase productivity and stay within budget. But on the emotional/human needs level they may want to cut down on the stress at work or go home on time. The person who seeks out both the logical and emotional/human needs will succeed over the person who meets only the logical need. In order to do this, you must learn to present both logical *and* emotional proofs.

For presentations, the formula is easy. First you need to decide what point you want to make. Then you must provide emotional proof, alternating with logical proof. And you can alternate them in any order.

For example:

1 Your point
2 Emotional proof
3 Logical proof

Or it could look like this:

1 Logical proof
2 Your point
3 Emotional proof

Or:

1 Emotional proof
2 Logical proof
3 Your point

How to develop logical proof

Let's look at logical proof first, not because it's more important, but because it's more familiar.

With logical proof you have several options. They include supporting your point as follows.

Three methods of logical proof

1 Numbers and statistics
2 References
3 Quotations from experts

Numbers and statistics have power

Let's look at some examples:

'When we changed to the new machinery, we needed three fewer employees for the same productivity,' the manager said.

SUNDAY
MONDAY
TUESDAY
WEDNESDAY
THURSDAY
FRIDAY
SATURDAY

'According to research, when children are six years old, 90% of them have an "I can do it" attitude towards learning. By the time they are 12, only 10% still have the "I can do it" attitude,' said the psychologist to the student teachers. As you see, this has much more impact with the statistics, rather than saying, *'We need teachers who encourage children.'* People need proof, and statistics make powerful proofs.

When you use statistical proof, be sure that your sentence *compares* the results. You can compare the results to another method *or* to the situation that existed prior to the change.

Don't say: *'This orange juice has 20% more vitamin C.'* This is a false claim because the '20% more' is compared to nothing. The listener asks *'20% more than what?'* Do say: *'This orange juice has 20% more vitamin C than Brand X,'* or, *'This orange juice from today's crop has 20% more vitamin C than orange juice made from the crop of five days ago.'*

Of course, the percentage or number you quote must be true.

Now let's look at how to use references to create proof and persuasion.

References for persuasion

Just as you learned how to use personal credibility prefaces in the last chapter, you can use references to another person or group as a credibility preface for your point. Here are some examples:

'George Schmidt from company ABC says that the method I'm going to tell you about saved his business.' (Then make your point.)

'The award winning football team for seven consecutive seasons, always practised the method that we're speaking about today.' (Then make your point.)

Quotations from experts lend credibility

When you want to make personal impact and have your points accepted it's beneficial to use a quote from an expert. Make sure that your audience, be it one or many, know and respect the person you are quoting. The use of quotes by respected authorities adds credibility to your statement.

'John Oppenheimer, the Nobel Prize winner, said, "This method helped me more than anything in my career."'

'Karl Kantor, world expert in fire fighting said, "If you follow the procedure that you see on the film coming up, you'll save your own life and the lives of others."'

TIP

Perfecting 'logical proof' impact

1 *Think of a point you want to make.*
2 *Think about the three possible forms of logical proof you could choose from*

   a) *numbers and statistics*
   b) *references to another person or group*
   c) *quotations from experts*

3 *Choose which to use, either actual or hypothetical for now.*
4 *Jot down your choice, with the actual words you would use. Later you can refer to this for ideas.*

How to develop emotional proof

With emotional proof you can use this formula. Develop a true story based on your life experience, if possible, because it's the most effective. Also, no one can refute it as it is your experience and no one else's. Alternatively, you can also use another person's true story if it is powerful.

1 **WHEN** did it happen?
2 **WHERE** did it happen?
3 **WHAT** happened?

Here are some examples:

   When did it happen? You can state it in several ways:
   'Yesterday ...'
   'Last Tuesday ...'
   'When I was 21 ...'
   'In 2011 ...'
   Where did it happen?
   'I was at the world trade conference ...'

'I was sitting at my desk ...'
'I stood in the doorway ...'
'We were walking from the elevator to my office ...'
What happened?
'Suddenly the boss walked up and said ...'
'I saw the most amazing sight in the sky. It looked ...'
'At that very instant, she slammed the report down on my desk ...'
'I realized for the first time in my life that ...'

Now try it for yourself. Here's an example of linking childhood stories to points in management to help spark your ideas:

'When I was seven, I was playing on a swing with the neighbour's child who was five. She jumped off and the swing hit her on the head. My father thought it was my fault and punished me. That taught me an important lesson. Now, even in management, I try never to blame an employee or colleague for anything until I hear their side of the story.'

Notice the use the three parts of the formula:
(When) *'When I was seven ...'*
(Where) *'I was playing on a swing ...'*
(What) – now your story.

Create memory value

Compare the impact of the story above to simply lecturing about management with something like this. *'Never blame an employee for anything without hearing their side of the story.'* It holds no 'memory value' because it is missing the emotional content. When you want to make personal impact and have your points remembered, there is hardly anything more powerful than a personal story.

Don't hold yourself back by wondering if you have the 'right' incident or a 'good' incident. The important thing is to practise the when, where, what, until it flows easily.

Perfecting 'emotional proof' impact

1 Think of an incident from your life experience and a lesson it taught you. It could have happened yesterday or years ago.

2 Develop three sentences to make your story. Use the three part formula.

a. When:

b. Where:

c. What:

3 Good. When it starts to flow, it shouldn't take you more than 30 seconds to develop such a story. In the beginning it will take you much longer. Again, don't worry about what's right.

Now let's develop the *point* segment of your impact formula.

Know your point – make your point!

Have you ever listened to anyone – your spouse, your best friend, your doctor, your politician – and wondered, 'What's the point, what are you trying to get at?'

If you want to hold the attention of your listeners, know your point and make your point. You may even need to repeat it more than once.

Remember, *your listener doesn't know where you are heading*, nor does he have all your background and expertise. Don't assume that your point is too obvious to mention. *Never leave your point to chance.* You have to give it to them straight.

There's no rule that says you can't make the point at the beginning and again at the end after your emotional and logical proof. It would look like this:

- Your point
- *Emotional Proof*
- *Logical Proof*
- Your point

For example:

'*Thank you, Margaret, for your introduction. Good morning everyone. Today I'm going to make an important point about warning your children about the misuse of drugs in society.* (This is your point.)

In 2010, I was travelling from London to New York, when I met an expert who told me ... (This is your emotional proof story.)

Research shows that 83% of all youngsters between the ages of 10 and 16 ... [This is your logical proof statistic.]

The point is that we as parents must warn our children about the misuse of drugs in our society. It is our responsibility. It is not an option. If you don't want your children to succumb to drugs, you must talk with them tonight and not delay.' [This is your point again.]

Or you could start immediately with your emotional proof, then the logical proof, then the point. *'Thank you ... Good morning ... In 2010, I was travelling ...'*

Alternatively, you could start immediately with your logical proof. *'Thank you ... Good morning ... Research shows that 83% of all ...'* then the emotional proof, then the point.

Whichever way you decide to do it, you must know your point and state your point! State it clearly and succinctly, before and/or after your proofs.

Put yourself in the listeners' shoes. They are bombarded by words, words, words, and more words. Their minds are racing, trying to deduce your point. When you say *'The point is ...'* it's a relief to your listener's mind.

Structure your presentation – for high impact

Winston Churchill was once told, 'If you are a Parliamentarian you can make one point. If you are a Minister, you can make two points. If you are the Prime Minister, you can make three points.'

I'm afraid there are many of us – bosses, managers, parents, teachers, experts and presenters of all disciplines – who forget that. The fact is that we can be much more effective if we make one point, and one point only. By that I mean we should have one message. *All points, and their connected proofs, serve to establish and strengthen one message.*

Below you'll find a tool I've created for our Effective Presentation Seminars, called the Circular 'Impact Formula' Chart. You'll find this tool not only effective for presentations, but also for any point you want to prepare for a meeting, a talk with the boss or staff members, or any other time you want to make high impact.

Here's an example of how to use it. One of my favourite messages is about the need to use positivity in our lives and our businesses. That's my message. Then I have several points and connected proofs to show why it's important and how to do it. The structure will look like the chart below, or have similar variations.

As you look at the diagram below, imagine the presentation you might make. In the centre is the main message you want to deliver. Mine, in this case, is 'Use positivity for results in management'.

After you choose your main message, think of five or more points that support your message. In my points below, I have three showing why my message is important, one showing how *not* to do it and one showing how *to* do it, all with supporting proofs.

Note that in my point six, I actually give two logical proofs to support my point along with one emotional proof – a personal story. The two logical proofs might be a statistic along with a reference for persuasion or a quote for credibility.

My final point under point six is a call to action. As in my previous example, a call to action would sound like this: 'If you want X, then you must do Y without delay.' The specific words in that example were: 'If you don't want your children to succumb to drugs, you must talk with them tonight and not delay.'

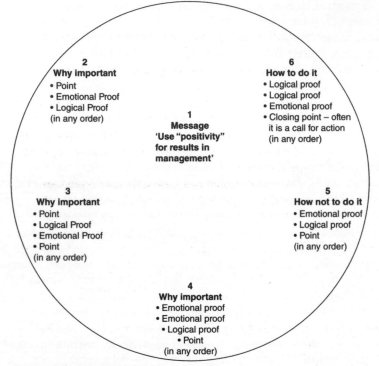

Circular 'impact formula' chart

The exciting part of this impact formula is the flexibility you have to design it according to your field, your profession and your personality. By adding as many logical and emotional proofs as you like, always remembering to make your point clearly before and/or after the proofs, you have a fool-proof formula. It's a matter of multiplying your points and related proofs: both logical and emotional, making sure they all support your message.

Take a moment now to structure a talk of your own. Pick a topic from your business, your life or your community. Pick something you feel strongly about, perhaps product potential, the economy, the environment, etc. It can be a talk you really need to give, or a hypothetical one. Either one is excellent preparation. Use the questions in the Tip Box below to formulate your thoughts, before creating your own Circular Impact Chart.

TIP
....
Impact Journal

Structure a talk now, point by point in your impact journal, using the Circular Impact Formula above as a guideline.

1 *What is the main message you want to get across?* _____

2 *Now your 1ˢᵗ supporting point, and proofs in any order*

3 *Now your 2ⁿᵈ supporting point, and proofs in any order*

4 *Now your 3ʳᵈ supporting point, and proofs in any order*

5 *Continue with as many points and supporting proofs as you wish*

6 *Now your closing point. Restate your main message, and the suggested action that should be taken.*
....

Congratulations. If you have to get up on your feet tomorrow and give a presentation, you will do a fine job with this structure. You can rest assured that you will be perceived as a professional, and your points will be taken seriously.

Make smooth transitions

After you become proficient at choosing your points and proofs, you'll want to think about 'transitions'. How will you switch from one story or point to another? How will you give your audience a clue that you are changing to a new point? Transitions let the 'computer of their mind' store the new point in a new place in the brain, thus not merging or confusing the two stories.

One way to do it is with a *pause*. You can give your first point and proof, then pause, then start your new point and proof. For example, the point could be '*... The lesson I learned from that incident is that people are not motivated by money alone.*' PAUSE '*Research proves ...*'. (Make your next proof.)

Another way to do it is with a *linking sentence*. State your incident/story, then say: '*After that incident, I started to research the subject and I discovered that...*'. (This is your transition to the next point, the research finding such as a statistic, which is your logical proof.)

Don't make the mistake of making your transition sentence too long or complicated. If you do, you'll lose your listeners. It's better to have a nice solid pause, than to fill your speech with words that serve no purpose.

Remember the lesson we learn from film producers and script writers who make every word and every scene count. Each has a purpose and leads to the plot. Nothing is extraneous. We must do the same in our presentations.

Social media application

If you are making a video for any purpose including YouTube, or if you are recording for internet radio, there is nothing more powerful for proving your points than the logical and emotional methods of proof contained in this chapter.

Draw upon numbers and statistics to make your point stick in the mind of your viewers. The same is true for readers or listeners. Draw upon your background for stories that you can use to make an emotional/human impact link to your point.

When using quotes or references, make absolutely sure that your quote is accurate. No one wants to be quoted wrongly, and neither do we. The best way to build followers and a positive support base is by giving accurate credit where credit is due. And when deciding on your content, remember to utilize the Circular Impact Formula in this chapter. Decide on your main message, list your points to support your message, and support your points with your high impact stories, stats, numbers, quotes and references.

Summary

This chapter provided you with the Circular Impact Formula – an easy and powerful way to structure your presentations. The key to having a memorable talk is providing proof for the listener – both logical and emotional proofs. Both are essential to high impact. Both are necessary to reach the left and right hemispheres of the listener's brain regardless of the subject.

For logical proofs you learned about three exceptionally powerful sources. Those are statistics, references for persuasion and quotes that lend credibility. For emotional proofs, we need to reach back through our experiences in life and select personal stories that link with our points, our audience, and our profession. Your list of background points from the last chapter can serve as a valuable source for personal stories.

The Circular Impact Formula allows you to combine your main message, points and proofs into a powerful presentation. You also learned two ways to transition from point to point, including a pause or a linking

SUNDAY

MONDAY

TUESDAY

WEDNESDAY

THURSDAY

FRIDAY

SATURDAY

sentence. These transitions give the mind of the listener a clue that your next point is coming. The Circular Impact Formula allows you to get on your feet tomorrow if necessary and deliver a memorable talk with the highest of professionalism.

Fact-check (answers at the back)

1. When we deliver a message, we must provide proof to our listeners. Which of the following is true?
   a) Logical proof is the most important ❑
   b) Emotional proof is the most important ❑
   c) They are equally important ❑
   d) Neither is important ❑

2. When making the proofs for our points, we should
   a) make our logical point first ❑
   b) make our emotional point first ❑
   c) make them in either order ❑
   d) make the logical proof after the point ❑

3. Numbers and statistics have power because they appeal to the logical side of the brain. Which is true below?
   a) These proofs always need a percentage ❑
   b) These proofs always need a number ❑
   c) These proofs can provide either ❑
   d) These proofs don't need to be accurate ❑

4. Another method of logical proof is to refer to a well-known person and show that they
   a) agree with our point ❑
   b) disagree with our point ❑
   c) know you well ❑
   d) know your company well ❑

5. A third way to give logical proof is to
   a) quote a fortune cookie ❑
   b) quote an expert ❑
   c) quote the most attractive person at the meeting ❑
   d) quote a fictitious magazine ❑

6. When giving emotional proof, it's possible to relay a story from what source?
   a) From your personal life experience ❑
   b) From your personal career experience ❑
   c) From either of the above ❑
   d) From none of the above ❑

7. Three points should be used to make a story powerful. They include:
   a) When, where, what ❑
   b) Who, where, when ❑
   c) She, he, they ❑
   d) Why, where, when ❑

8. When making your point, it's important to verbalize it, and not assume that your listener will catch it. The best time to state your point is
   a) before your emotional proof ❑
   b) before your logical proof ❑
   c) at the beginning AND end of your proofs ❑
   d) any of the above ❑

SUNDAY MONDAY TUESDAY WEDNESDAY THURSDAY FRIDAY SATURDAY

9. Winston Churchill was once given advice we should all follow. He was told that if you are a Parliamentarian, and not a Prime Minister, you should make how many points each time you speak?
a) Three ❏
b) Two ❏
c) One ❏
d) Any of the above ❏

10. If you want to inspire your audience to take a certain action based on your presentation, you should state that action succinctly at what part of your talk?
a) Beginning ❏
b) Middle ❏
c) End ❏
d) Any of the above ❏

SUNDAY

MONDAY

TUESDAY

WEDNESDAY

THURSDAY

FRIDAY

SATURDAY

WEDNESDAY

Make your point stick using incidents, analogies, and humour

Listen to a small child talking to his parents, 'Tell me a story, tell me a story.'

The love of stories never leaves a person. Stories are listened to. Statements are ignored. Stories are remembered. Statements are forgotten.

'A picture is worth a thousand words.' When you relay an incident, you are painting a mental picture for your listener.

These mental pictures touch the hearts of listeners and help them remember. If you can touch the emotions of people, your message stays indelibly ingrained on them. You make your point stick.

The purpose of this chapter is to lead you away from ineffective presentations and ineffective personal impact. You will learn to drop the notion of using filler words, and go straight to that which is effective – the incident or story, analogies and even humour.

In this chapter you will learn how to:

Use high impact stories and incidents for maximum results
Make your messages memorable with analogies
Use humour to your advantage

Use incidents for high impact

I remember one speaking engagement early in my career in which I was the third speaker. The conference theme was technical, dealing with proposed changes in British legislation. I prepared by studying the government 'white paper' on the subject, and then I developed my stories and proofs.

However, the two people who preceded me gave very traditional talks. They read from their papers, they had all facts, no analogies or stories – nothing to make their points stick. I started to get cold feet. 'Should I change my presentation?' I wondered. 'Perhaps I should just give facts too and drop the stories, analogies and humour.' I remember struggling with myself about what to do, but at last I decided to stick with my plan.

I delivered my speech *with* the stories. Can you guess how the audience reacted? They loved it. And the proof of the success is that the organization invited me back – not once, but three times. My point is this. If you want to have high impact and have your points remembered, don't change your plan. Use stories and incidents no matter what the other presenters do.

Influence decisions

Whether you're speaking to people one to one, in a management meeting, or giving a presentation, your goal should be to formulate incidents or high impact stories, so that you can influence decision making. *That's the essence of personal impact.*

Always remember
Stories are listened to, but statements are ignored.
Stories are remembered, but statements are forgotten.

Think of each sentence you create as a brush stroke. You're painting a scene in an animated movie. First you have to set the scene, as you studied in the Tuesday chapter for emotional proof. Today you'll be applying it to make your point stick. As you remember, it's best to state the when and where before you state what happened.

Think of the *WHEN* and the *WHERE* as the container of your *WHAT* action, just as a tea cup is the container of tea. If you pour tea out without having a container, it will spill in all directions making a mess. It will be useless to the drinkers.

The same is true of your story. If you pour out the action part without the *WHEN* and *WHERE* container, there will be no place in the listener's mind for the *WHAT* action to fall. It will make a mess in the mind rather than being contained in its proper mental compartment for proper impact.

Show *WHEN* it was; *'day, night, yesterday, last week, two years ago.'* Second you show *WHERE* it was; *'inside, outside, in a car, in a building, standing by a desk.'* Now your listener has his mental picture into which he can put the action – the *WHAT* of our story.

Now you can tell what happened; *'my boss said to me..., or, suddenly I realized..., or, she tripped in front of my eyes...'.*

Magnetic effect of incidents/stories

Think of small children again. They are energetic. When they talk and when they run, they ooze out energy. We adore them, we admire them. It draws us to them like a magnet. The same is true with presenters. Listeners are drawn to energy and vitality. You can have it too when you use high impact stories.

And don't use them sparingly. I remember teaching my trainers about the power of personal incidents and stories. They all learned quickly using the formulas in this chapter. They could stand up and deliver a perfect incident/story, with incredible skill. But when I heard them deliver an entire presentation, I was shocked. I realized that I had made a big mistake. I hadn't told them to start their speech with a story. I hadn't told them to make every point with a story. I hadn't told them to end with a story. I hadn't told them that their speech should be a string of stories with proofs or analogies.

I discovered they thought they should just insert a story here and there to accent it, similar to the way jewellery accents a garment. If we go out without earrings or a tie clip, the world doesn't come to an end. That's how they viewed stories.

I don't want you to make the same mistake. Stories and incidents should not accent your speeches, they should *be* your speech. This is true whether you are addressing a medical convention, educators, business colleagues or Parliament.

Why do I give you this advice? The answer is simple. If you make each point with a story, people will listen. If you don't, they won't. Which do you want?

I know at first this is hard to believe. You may be used to hearing people speak without stories and incidents. But do you remember what they said? Probably not.

I was once interviewed on radio in London. The interviewer was tough and had a worldwide reputation for turning callers and guests into mincemeat if they seemed the slightest bit unprepared or illogical.

I was told that I would have six minutes to present my case on a controversial issue, and then the interviewer and the callers would be turned loose to let me self-destruct. Anyone who was invited to be interviewed on this show was thought to be terribly 'gutsy'.

Here's how I prepared. I drew a line down the centre of my paper. I made a list of points I wanted to make in the left column. In the right column I put a list of high impact stories that made my point. I used credibility prefaces such as: *'When I met Prince Charles I made this point about marketing in Great Britain....'* And *'When I was Chair of the London Chamber of Commerce...'*

When the show was over I had many congratulatory phone calls from people who I hadn't seen for years. It was a wonderful experience, due to preparation and reliance on high impact stories and incidents.

TIP *No one can argue with personal experience. You own it. It's yours.*

You might be tempted to think you can't use stories in business or in high powered situations. Not true.

As an example, here is how I started my speech to the Parliament of Czechoslovakia after Communism dissolved, in 1990, on the subject of Privatization of Industry: *'Yesterday in Prague, I was training a group of senior managers in the subject of...'* (Note the *WHEN, WHERE* and *WHAT* format. Note also that the *WHERE* part of the story has high impact because it takes place in their country, giving credibility to the story.)

Then I talked about uncertainty, which was the issue at hand for them at this difficult time of transition away from Communism: *'The point of the story is this: When we are working in uncharted waters, we can never be sure of what results we can get. We can do research, we can debate, we can take an educated guess, but in the end, we have to start some place.'*

My 45 minute address consisted of 20 incidents to support my point, which was to speed up the passage of their Privatization Bill. I ended with this story. *'My grandparents left Prague to immigrate to America looking for greener pastures. Today your country has the opportunity to be the greener pasture. There are 16 million people here right now, ready and willing to move forward with you...*

'... In closing, I repeat my point. The country waits for you. The world waits for you. History waits for you. As you leave here today, keep with you the passion to be focused – not on the problems but on the solutions – in order to pass the Privatization Bill without delay.' (Note the use of the words 'in closing' to focus their attention on my final 'call for action' power closing: 'to pass the Privatization Bill without delay.')

What's my point? If you want to succeed even in the most formal circumstances, use stories and incidents as the building blocks of your presentation. If every story has a point, and all points support your message, then your presentation is done. You're ready to fly. Make your stories and incidents the meat of your talk, *not* an accessory.

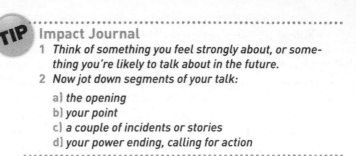

TIP Impact Journal

1 *Think of something you feel strongly about, or something you're likely to talk about in the future.*

2 *Now jot down segments of your talk:*

 a) *the opening*
 b) *your point*
 c) *a couple of incidents or stories*
 d) *your power ending, calling for action*

Now you're ready for more embellishments. Let's look at how to make your messages more memorable with analogies and humour.

Analogies – for memorable messages

What is an analogy? It's actually something totally unrelated to your point, yet you draw a comparison to it. Does that sound strange? Well, it is. That's why we remember analogies when we hear them. And that's what you want from your listeners.

It's the same principle that humourists use. They take something ordinary from life and do the unexpected with it. That's why we laugh.

Analogies call on the unexpected too, but they don't provoke humour, they provoke our memory. Analogies can seem odd at first, but after you try it and see the effect it has on your listeners, you'll never turn back.

Now, let's apply analogies to concepts you may want to convey. To create an analogy, you simply need two things:

1 A concept you want to convey
2 An object for comparison

Let's say that John, a new manager, wants to impress this concept upon his employees: *'It's imperative to be here on time each morning.'*

Now he chooses an object for his analogy. He looks around the office and chooses 'carpet'. Now he'll link 'carpet' to being on time each morning.

Speaking to his employees he says: *'I want to draw your attention to our carpet. We know it protects the floor from scratches. In some ways it's like employees when they are on time. Being on time protects the company from losing business because the phones get answered, and customers place orders.*

'This provides work for the company and pay cheques for employees. If we want to protect our floor from scratches, we need a carpet. If we want to protect customers and employees, we have to be here on time each morning.'

In the example above, John considered the words 'ash tray' and 'window' for his analogy, and finally settled on 'carpet'. Any object can be used for a good analogy on any subject. It's just a matter of looking at it from different angles until you find one that fits.

Another time John's message is about good customer service. The object he chooses is 'magnet'. His analogy sounded like this: *'Do you notice how often people choose to go to sunny places for holidays? The sunshine seems to act like a magnet. They feel good and rejuvenated. However, if the sun doesn't shine, that's the first thing they complain about when they come back!*

'It's the same with customer service. If we are polite and helpful to customers, they keep coming back. Our helpfulness acts like a magnet. It makes them feel good. On the other hand if we are discourteous, they complain to everyone and we lose customers. Next time you deal with a customer, remember to be the magnet that keeps pulling them back.'

How often should you use analogies? Use them like accessories. If you have a 45 minute presentation, you might want to make your point with two or three analogies. Use them on the points that need highest impact.

TIP

Impact Journal
1 *Now think of a concept you want to communicate.*
2 *Pick an object.*
3 *Turn the object and the concept around in your mind. Where can you find a link? Use the two analogies above*

from John, the new manager, as an example. Try different objects until you find one you like.

4 *Then make the link to your concept and write it out. Keep it for future reference.*

Use analogies sparingly for the highest impact. I once heard two men on the radio speak for 15 minutes non-stop using analogy after analogy. They had no stories and no points. Just analogies. By the time they finished, the listeners' minds were in overdrive. My point is this. Definitely use analogies, but use them as a special treat for your listeners, not the main course.

In the Friday chapter, you'll find The Presentation Planning Matrix – a great tool to let you plan ahead for a good mix of analogies, stories, proofs and other component parts of good presentations. I've created this for our Effective Presentation Seminars to make presentation planning easier and more effective. With the matrix you can easily decide how many analogies to use and on which points to use them.

For now, let's move on to humour.

Use humour to your advantage

What about humour in the workplace? Have you ever been in a meeting in which tensions grew high? People feel uncomfortable, and no one knows quite what to say. At those moments, humour can save the day. And if you can use humour effectively, it can give you an edge over your competition. More importantly, humour can be used to make your point stick in the mind of your listeners, whether in a meeting or a presentation.

The essential thing to remember in the workplace is always to use humour positively, never at the expense of another person.

Since you've already studied analogies, you'll proceed to humour easily. The basis of humour is the unexpected. With analogies, you are taking two unrelated concepts and finding a comparison. With humour you'll take an incident or a word or phrase and find an unexpected twist. You point out something the others didn't see.

Begin by drawing on your own true life experiences and your success with humour will come easier. Here's a longer list you can also draw upon:

Humour can be thought of as a form of emotion. When your words or actions make people laugh, they are physically moved, not just mentally touched. This is what makes your message more firmly planted.

Perfecting the impact of humour

Look at the list above. Choose one of the categories and write down any situation as it actually happened, but then add a twist. Perhaps how someone else would have seen it – a stranger, or a Martian or your mother-in-law, or the school head master. Perhaps how it would look 50 years from now, or a hundred years ago.

Don't worry if it takes you some time.

Let your mind work on it, even overnight. The twist will come.

Remember, the twist is what makes people laugh because it is the unexpected.

Take a tip from professional humourists. They all worry about whether their lines will go over the first time. They just put the line out, pause, and hope!

You may find that the reverse is true too. You may deliver a serious line, which touches people as funny. That's all right. You can laugh too. Then go home and analyse it. You can even record your presentations to review later. Perhaps you can build on the laugh to make it bigger, or circle back to it later in the presentation for another laugh.

Good. You've worked through a lot of material on creating power and high impact. When you add stories, analogies, and humour, you are armed with tremendous power to use in your profession, in presentations and in leadership.

Social media application

The three tools of story, analogies and humour can be used in all social media, whether visual or text.

Practise making them short, sharp and crisp. In social media you will lose people quickly if you don't get to your point immediately. Don't be misguided by thinking that a story needs to be long. A story with a powerful point can be merely one sentence or two. The same is true for analogies and humour.

You might start like this. Write out your story, analogy or humour point. Then take an axe to it and cut out each and every extraneous word.

Like the film producer, make sure each word leads you to your point. Short and sharp. A two-minute video clip could contain six segments of 20-second stories, analogies and humour points. *That* is high impact.

Summary

The three tools of stories/incidents, analogies and humour are captivating ways to have high impact and set you apart from others on your career path. They make your message stick in the minds of your listeners. They can be used for influencing decision making whether you are speaking one to one, in a management meeting, or giving a presentation.

You learned that unlike statements, stories and incidents live long in the memory of our listeners. It's often said that a picture is worth a thousand words. Your story, or the relaying of an incident, is the painting of that picture.

Next you learned how to use analogies for the concepts you want to convey. An analogy, like humour, provides your listener with an unexpected twist. It links something quite unrelated to the concept you want them to remember, in an unexpected way.

Humour can be used in the workplace to take the edge off tension or to make your message stick. However, we must remember to never use humour at the expense of another person in order to avoid negative repercussions.

SUNDAY
MONDAY
TUESDAY
WEDNESDAY
THURSDAY
FRIDAY
SATURDAY

Fact-check (answers at the back)

1. The three methods of making your point stick are stories/incidents, analogies and humour. Which of them utilizes 'a twist'?
   a) Story or incident ❏
   b) Analogy ❏
   c) Humour ❏
   d) Both analogy and humour ❏

2. The mental pictures you create through relaying stories or incidents, do what to the listener?
   a) Help them remember ❏
   b) Touch their heart ❏
   c) Keep your message indelibly ingrained ❏
   d) All of the above ❏

3. Which of the following is true?
   a) Stories are listened to ❏
   b) Statements are forgotten ❏
   c) Stories are remembered ❏
   d) All of the above ❏

4. Stories and incidents should be used to make your point with the following groups:
   a) Business colleagues ❏
   b) A medical convention, educators, or Parliament ❏
   c) All of the above ❏
   d) None of the above ❏

5. The mistake I made when training my trainers about the effective use of stories and incidents was that I didn't tell them which of the following?
   a) To start every presentation with a story and proofs ❏
   b) To make every point with a story and a proof or analogy ❏
   c) To end with a story ❏
   d) All of the above ❏

6. An analogy contains which of the following?
   a) Something unrelated to your point, yet you can draw a comparison to it ❏
   b) It takes something ordinary from life and does the unexpected with it ❏
   c) It doesn't usually provoke humour, it provokes memory ❏
   d) All of the above ❏

7. To develop your own analogy, first think of a concept you want to convey. Second you pick an object to draw a comparison to. The object should be:
   a) Something sensible ❏
   b) Something outlandish ❏
   c) Something the listener can relate to ❏
   d) It could be anything ❏

8. Should analogies be like an accessory or the meat of a presentation? For example, in a 45-minute presentation, how many analogies are ideal?
a) One ☐
b) Two/three ☐
c) Five to seven ☐
d) At least 10 ☐

9. Sources for humour can come from where?
a) Life situations ☐
b) TV, articles, books ☐
c) Almost anything ☐
d) All of the above ☐

10. Humour is best used about harmless situations. If used at the expense of another person, it can
a) backfire on you ☐
b) hinder your career ☐
c) cause you to lose friends ☐
d) all of the above ☐

THURSDAY

Grasp 13 ways to 'grab and hold' attention

Anyone can address a group, providing they have the courage, but how many can grab and hold the attention of their listeners and have high impact? The answer is, not many.

More often than not, their openings are lacklustre. These include what we call the 'housekeeping' start, the 'apology' start, the 'humble speaker' start, and the 'ho-hum' start. These openings discourage your listeners, put them to sleep and make them wish they hadn't come. Don't let this happen to you. Instead, use dynamic openings and ways to grab attention immediately.

We must continue to hold attention throughout our presentations, whether in meetings at work, or in prestigious conferences of all sizes.

Today you'll learn 13 ways to grab attention in the beginning and hold it throughout the beginning, middle and end. These include:

Power openings

The use of questions – with and without answers

Audience participation

Using objects to hold the attention

Creating suspense

Power closings

Social media applications

Power openings

How often have you gone to a meeting or conference with high expectations, only to have those expectations dashed by a long or boring kick-off?

Just yesterday I heard this conference opening: 'I was just given this list 30 seconds ago by Jane, so don't blame me if I come across unprepared!' What a derogatory start! Firstly, it reflects badly on the speaker for not taking responsibility for preparing himself, and for blaming a colleague. Secondly, it reflects badly on Jane, his colleague. Thirdly, it reflects badly on his organization for not ensuring better preparation. And last but not least, it leaves the listeners totally discouraged and uninspired about what is to follow! This is a variation of the 'apology opening' which you'll read about soon.

Openings are best without preamble. Our purpose as presenters is to grab the attention of the listener immediately. Personally, I want to be able to hear a pin drop within 10 seconds of my opening words. You should aim for the same, even as a beginning presenter.

How can you do this? Go straight into your story/incident as you learned in the previous chapter. Let's say your subject is education. After thanking your introducer, you might say: 'My first child had tremendous problems at school reading and consequently ... '. By starting this way, you have grabbed your audience. They are now ready to hear more. Don't make the mistake of starting with: 'Tonight I want to speak about education, its advances, and its shortcomings. From the early part of the century ...'. That shouts 'boring, boring.' Today's audiences are used to quick-pace media and they want a quick start. If you feel it's important to state your topic, say it briefly after your personal story, once you have grabbed their attention.

Don't be guided by what is 'average' or 'normal' in other presentations you hear. Your purpose in reading this book is to be good or great, not average. And you *can* be great by going straight for the grabber opening, either with a personal incident or any one of the 13 'grab and hold' attention techniques listed for you in the box that follows.

13 Ways to 'grab and hold' attention

Start your speech with something exciting. Start with something that engages the listener's mind. A personal incident grabs their attention immediately. A question also gets their attention. There are many ways to start a presentation, whether it's around a meeting table or a conference room. You can draw upon any of these methods in order to create dynamic openings:

The first seven you learned about in previous chapters
 1 Incidents and stories
 2 Statistics and numbers
 3 Expert quotes
 4 Refer to a well-known source – usually a person, company or organization
 5 Refer to a credible journal or research source
 6 A personal credibility point
 7 Humour

The following are covered in this chapter

 8 Power openings
 9 Questions – with or without answers
 10 Audience participation
 11 Demonstrate or exhibit something
 12 Create suspense
 13 Power closings

These 13 can be used effectively *throughout* your presentation.

Now let's look at what *won't* get attention. These ways of starting will discourage your listeners, put them to sleep, and make them wish they hadn't come. They may make you chuckle as you read them, but believe me, these lacklustre and demeaning openings are going on every day, in every corner of the earth. Don't let it happen to you.

Don'ts

1 'The Housekeeping Opening'
It may sound like this: *'Good morning. Our first break will be at 10:00. If you need to make a call, try to wait until the break. The ladies' room is around the corner, down the hall on the right, the men's is ...'*

Instead, post the housekeeping details on the notice board or print them on a hand-out. Start immediately by talking about the exciting programme you have scheduled, how happy you are that these people are attending, and what positive results they can expect from the day.

2 'The Apology Opening'

It may sound like this: *'Good morning. Our speaker for today, the award-winning expert on 19th century art, Mr Clement Smith couldn't be here tonight. He had to fly to Italy to see the Pope. He's really a very sought after person as you can tell. We're all really disappointed about it, but Mr Jones said he would come and do his best.'*

Now do you think that we in the audience are really psyched up? No, we wish we had the original speaker after that build up. Instead you should introduce Mr Jones *properly* and mention *in passing* that 'Mr Smith regrets he can't be here but would like to join us another time.'

Find out what Mr Jones's qualifications are and say: *'Good morning. Our speaker for today has had an interest in 19th century art since 2002 when he was lucky enough to live in Italy in his position as Cultural Attaché. In addition, he studies ..., and did ... We are very pleased that he is able to join us today in place of Mr Smith to enlighten us about ... Please help me welcome Arthur Jones.'*

3 'The Humble Speaker Opening'

It may sound like this: *'Good morning. I was quite stunned when Elizabeth invited me to talk to you. I don't quite know why she thought I was qualified, but I'll do my best ... .'*

If you say this, you are discrediting your audience, saying that they are stupid to come and hear you. You might think it's humbling, but in fact it insults your listeners.

Instead, learn to prepare your own introduction in the next chapter and give this to the organizer to present before your talk.

4 'The Ho-Hum Opening'

It may sound like this: *'Good morning. I thought a lot about what I could speak to you about. I could concentrate on X ..., or I could tell you about Y ..., but then I considered Z ... , finally I thought ..., but then again ... .'*

By the time you've finished your first paragraph, the audience is asleep. Instead, start with your incident – story, emotional proof or logical proof, or credibility prefaces as you learned in the previous chapter, or one of the points below.

The question technique

Not all questions need to have answers. Often it's enough to let people internalize their answers. The best questions are ones in which people reflect on life. Or perhaps on the way they do things.

There are three ways to use questions to grab and hold the attention of your listeners in meetings and conferences

1 Reflective questions, in which people internalize their answers
2 The 'show of hands' question
3 The 'verbal answer' question

The reflective question

It might sound like this: *'I'm going to ask you a question. Just reflect on the answer to yourself. How many teachers ... ?'*

This process is good as an opening, or for very thought-provoking issues later in a presentation. Often you don't want to break the emotional feeling you've created within people. If instead, you had people waving their hands around, it would break the focus. By having them internalize the answer, you can move them to a deeper level of thought or prepare them for your message to come.

This method is also good when you want people to think or reflect on what you've covered so far but you don't want to take time out for answers. For example, I use it effectively in workshops. I might say, *'What's the point we're trying to make in this module?'* Pause. Then I answer it. *'The point is ... .'*

In this way, a question can serve as a reflective think period, a mental review. It's important to give your listeners some time for mental review so that they can consolidate your material, before moving to your next plateau of ideas or points.

The reflective question is also good when people could be embarrassed by revealing the answer. It allows them to reflect without committing.

The 'show of hands' question

Questions with 'show of hands' answers serve to get the audience involved. When they have to answer, they have to think. The process helps to focus their minds and helps to get their support.

Examples could be: *'How many of you have ever tried this?'* Or: *'Put your hand up if you ever tried this.'* Be sure to tell the audience *before* your question that they will hold up their hands after the question.

Questions with 'show of hands' answers can also get commitment. For example, *'Put your hand up if you think you COULD use this.'* I sometimes take it further and ask a second question: *'Put your hand up if you WILL use it.'*

I'm always careful to only do this with a group which is already behind an idea. If you were to use it on an issue that people were not supporting, they would feel pressure and not like it. A boss couldn't use it, for example, to get employees to support their own goals with which the employees disagree, without causing resentment.

It's good to use the 'show of hands' question technique to prove a point. *'How many of you have experienced such and such?'* By doing that you involve the audience, you prove your point, and you don't alienate anyone.

The 'verbal answer' question

When soliciting verbal answers from your group, the important thing to remember is that the person is taking a risk by answering. The last thing they want is to look foolish in front of their peers, or in front of strangers, or in front of you. They don't like it when you ask them a question, and then tell them that their answer is *wrong*. I've watched speakers do this. It's the shortest path to sudden death. It's up to you *not* to let this happen.

Instead, handle it like this. Ask questions that don't have wrong and right answers. For example: *'Who will tell us what methods of success they use in this area?'* It's their method. It works for them. You congratulate them. You can also move on until you get the answer you are seeking.

It might sound like this, *'Here's the problem, what do you think causes this problem?'* You can even put answers on display. You can continue to pull answers until you get to the ones you want. In this way you never need to say *'Wrong'*, just *'Thank you, what else?'* Then you or the group can decide on the best answer and the virtues of it.

Good, now let's move on to other aspects of getting the audience involved.

Audience participation

I remember fondly one of our courses on Effective Presentations. Each person was deciding how to use audience participation to fit their topic. Suddenly I saw two people down on their knees, waving their arms around, holding out their trouser legs as though wind was blowing through them. It was an incredible sight. They really looked as though they were flying.

I went over and discovered they were demonstrating the art of parachute jumping! One was the speaker. The other was an audience 'volunteer' who the speaker had chosen to assist in demonstrating the excitement of parachute jumping. We were all captivated by the sight, waiting with bated breath to hear more.

The point is that audiences love participation. They feel that the audience member who goes to the front represents them. It has a uniting affect. They see their 'representative' interacting with you and it creates a bond and closeness between you and the audience. And you don't have to be an experienced speaker to get results with it.

In your presentations, you can bring an audience member up to accentuate any point. For example, during my motivational presentations I might ask an audience member to join me at the front and tell us about what they want to achieve. Perhaps improvements in productivity, or sales or morale building. Then they say what they plan to do to get the required results. I know from experience that my message sticks with my audience ten times more effectively by using audience participation. This will be true for you too.

Impact Journal

Take a moment now to think about ways you can use audience participation in your next presentation.

Where can you use it?

When can you use it?

How can you use it?

What results would you like to achieve?

Jot this down in your impact journal while it's fresh in your mind. In the future you can refer to it when you need it.

Using an object to hold attention

If you want to make a real impact on your audience, show an object. You might change their lives. In a meeting I attended long ago, the presenter held up a book about property investment.

He said, *'This book changed my life – the principles in here really work.'* I can still see that man in front of our group, holding that book up. It's as clear as if it was yesterday. I was so motivated that I went out and bought that book. And indeed, it changed my life too.

I'll always be grateful to that man. Why is that? It's because he got my attention and my interest. If he hadn't held that book up as an exhibit, his talk would not have been as powerful. My life would not have been affected.

Using objects to make your point is effective, whether you use them at the beginning, the middle or the end of your presentation. It's just as effective at work in a small meeting as it is in a large conference.

Let's look at some objects you can use:

Effective objects to grab and hold attention	
Book	Blank paper you mark on during speech
Map	Enlarged photograph
Chart	Diploma
Graph	Plaque
Report	Object (chair, instrument, machinery,
Newspaper	sport item, business item)
Magazine	Other (list your own ideas)
Computer printout	

Well done. Now let's move on to holding your audience in suspense. It is a very powerful aspect of speech making.

Create suspense

A promise plants the idea that something important is coming later *and* keeps your listener alert for it. It holds attention.

For example you could say: *'Later tonight I'm going to give you the exact secret of success told to me by the world's top sales performers. But first, let's look at ... .'*

Or you could start an intriguing story, but not don't finish it at that moment. You intersperse your other points, then come back to the story later. The listeners know you will come back to it, or at least hope you will, and thus stay in suspense waiting.

You can create the same effect with props and exhibits. For example, you can have something near you and either not mention it, or you can say that you'll come back to it later. That holds suspense too.

For example, I once used a long rope in this way. Two colleagues carried it to the stage, one holding each end. We rolled it up and put a blanket over it. I told the audience we would use it later, I didn't mention it again until a point late in my talk. Then we stretched the rope across the front of the room, horizontally, about 3 feet above the floor and used it as 'the line of demarcation' between negativity and positivity that we must cross in order to bring success into our lives. The audience never forgot it, and were still talking about it months later. Using a promise or suspense to hold attention is an effective way to get your point across and make it memorable.

Think now about how you can use a promise or suspense to hold attention. The list is endless, and no doubt you will think of others that relate to points you intend to convey.

Examples of creating suspense

- An important point you promise to give later
- Part of a story you promise to finish later
- An important quotation, secret, statistic or method you promise to give later
- An exhibit you promise to show later
- A demonstration you promise to do later
- A chance for them to participate later
- A person for them to meet later
- Part of a point, story or any of the above, which you start but don't finish, thus leaving the audience in suspense, knowing you'll come back to it

 Impact Journal

First, imagine any topic you might speak about.

Second, think of a promise you could hold out for the audience.

List these in your journal.

Now let's move on to one of the most important aspects of your presentation, powerful closings.

Power closings

Closings are best when they call for action and tell the audience what benefit they'll get by carrying out the action. For example, *'Remember that 90% of the people who write their*

goals down, achieve them. Go home tonight and do it. As the research shows, taking two minutes to write your goals down brings success.'

You can preface your closing with the words: *'In closing, ...'* if you like the feeling it brings. Some researchers believe that the ears of the audience pick up when they hear the words 'in closing'. However, then you must close, preferably within two to five sentences. If you talk longer, they will feel that you've not delivered on your promise, and your entire talk can be discredited. The simpler your close, the better. They've heard a lot from you. Now is the time to tell them what action to take and what results they can expect. Simple. Clear. Precise. You are telling them what they can do now to achieve the results you have discussed.

Social media application

The concept of powerful openings and closings can be used in both text formats and video formats. The same is true with the methods of grabbing and holding attention. So whether it's Facebook or YouTube or anything in the social media spectrum, use these principles to your advantage.

On YouTube, for example, a tremendous amount can be achieved in two or three minutes. If you prefer longer, that's great too. Remember that your viewers' needs are the same as those at work. They will tune you out if you have fatally boring openings and can't hold their attention throughout.

So make use of the reflective questions in which they can internalize their answers. Make use of audience participation by recruiting a volunteer to be taped with you. Make use of objects and promises to hold attention. When you do, your followers will multiply.

Summary

In this chapter you learned about the difference between a powerful opening and a lacklustre opening to your presentations. One puts people to sleep. The other energizes them. One makes people wish they hadn't come. The other raises their participation and positive results.

On the 'don't' side are trite and outdated openings such as housekeeping points, apologies, discrediting oneself, and the boring unprepared rambler.

Equally important are the 13 methods for grabbing and holding attention. The list of options includes the use of questions – with or without answers, audience participation, exhibits and objects, plus suspense or a promise of something you'll divulge later. All of these can be used quickly and effectively to grab and hold attention at the beginning, end and throughout your presentation for high impact.

Power closings are essential and are best when they call for action from the listener.

SUNDAY

MONDAY

TUESDAY

WEDNESDAY

THURSDAY

FRIDAY

SATURDAY

Fact-check (answers at the back)

1. In opening your presentation, you want to grab the attention of your listeners immediately. In fact, you should be able to hear a pin drop, within how many minutes or seconds of your opening?
   a) 10 seconds ❏
   b) 30 seconds ❏
   c) one minute ❏
   d) three minutes ❏

2. The best way to grab attention immediately is to
   a) tell a story or incident related to your message ❏
   b) start with the history of your subject ❏
   c) announce the break times ❏
   d) deliver a long preamble ❏

3. An 'excuse opening' has what downfalls?
   a) It reflects badly on the speaker ❏
   b) It reflects badly on the person being blamed ❏
   c) It reflects badly on the organization ❏
   d) All of the above ❏

4. In closing your presentation, you can use words such as 'In closing ... .' This re-engages your listeners to hear your final point. When using this closing, you should come to a close within
   a) the next sentence ❏
   b) one to five sentences ❏
   c) three to five minutes ❏
   d) ten minutes ❏

5. All bad openings have what in common?
   a) They leave your listeners discouraged ❏
   b) They leave your listeners uninspired about what is to follow ❏
   c) They leave your listeners bored ❏
   d) All of the above ❏

6. Using reflective questions is very good for
   a) thought provoking issues ❏
   b) allowing people to reflect on what you've covered ❏
   c) not embarrassing people by requiring a verbal response ❏
   d) all of the above ❏

7. Using questions is an excellent way to grab and hold attention. Why is this true?
   a) Questions break the ice ❏
   b) They bring variety to your talk ❏
   c) They change the pace ❏
   d) All of the above ❏

8. Some of the world's greatest presenters use the technique of audience participation for high impact. By bringing a member of the audience to the front to interact with you, the other audience members feel what?
   a) Represented ❏
   b) Afraid ❏
   c) Resentful ❏
   d) Threatened ❏

9. Using objects in your presentation is a highly effective way to hold attention. It is most effective if used when?

a) At the beginning ☐
b) In the middle ☐
c) At the end ☐
d) Any and all of the above ☐

10. A promise plants the idea that something important is coming later and keeps your listener alert for it. Some examples are:

a) Start an intriguing story, but finish it later ☐
b) Promise to show an exhibit later ☐
c) Pose a question and promise to answer it later ☐
d) All of the above ☐

FRIDAY

Build your fool-proof 'Presentation Planning Matrix'

Now we come to the time for the ultimate decision – what points will you include in your meeting or presentation? What points do you want to hammer home? What result do you want for your listeners?

Now it's time to let your creative juices flow. Which of the methods will you use to prove your points? Emotional proof stories, logical proof statistics, analogies, humour – what will you choose?

And how will you open and close your presentation? Will you avoid the typical lacklustre start and go for a power opening? A power close? Which of the 13 methods of grabbing and holding attention will you use? This is the moment to take everything you've learned, and like a puzzle, pull all the pieces together as you like it.

In this chapter you'll be given a magnificent tool, the 'Presentation Planning Matrix', to help you put the puzzle pieces together with both ease and high impact. This matrix allows you to:

Choose your main message

Plot the points to support your message

Time your message appropriately

Gear your points to your listeners for high impact

Know what to do when invited to speak

Use social media applications

Benefits of the 'Presentation Planning Matrix'

No one said it's easy to get your points across effectively. In conferences and meetings, people rarely put their points across well. Instead, they often mumble their thoughts to each other as they leave the room. This is negative for the organization because the best ideas stay hidden from discussion. Thus decisions are made without the best talent and ideas coming forward.

The second thing you'll notice about meetings and conferences is the timing. Rarely does a conference, or even a high level Board of Directors meeting, end on time. Seldom do people know how to time their presentations and still incorporate all their points.

Fortunately, this won't happen to you. Why? Because you'll have our fool-proof Presentation Planning Matrix that you can use to plan your presentation. As you'll see below, it aids you in choosing your main message, plus your points and proofs to support it. It also allows you to add variety to 'grab and hold' attention, thus utilizing all you've learned to do in previous chapters. By utilizing these methods, you'll have a high impact presentation and, best of all, you'll develop it with ease and confidence.

And there's one more important ingredient in the matrix. It's your timing! The brilliance of the matrix is that by choosing your specific points, proofs, etc., you'll be able to time each one so that your finished presentation fits the requirements of the meeting or conference.

SUNDAY
MONDAY
TUESDAY
WEDNESDAY
THURSDAY
FRIDAY
SATURDAY

Sample of 'The Matrix'

Let's have a look now at a sample of the filled-in 'Presentation Planning Matrix'. This is a sample of one I used myself for a 45-minute motivational conference presentation. Use this as a model. Next you'll have a chance to fill in your own.

PRESENTATION PLANNING MATRIX MY MAIN MESSAGE: YOU CAN DO IT						
Point	Emotional proof Personal Incident Story	Time	Logical Proof Statistic/Quote/ Reference	Time	Analogy Demonstration/ Participation/ Question	Time
Neg/Pos.	Airplane Story	4	Children 6–12	2		
	Lady LA	2			Pebbles in a Pond.	6
			Expert Journal	2		
Dolphin method	Management Incident Mercedes.	2				
	Home incident Tom	4				
	Management Song	2				
			Pearson Whistle	2		
Catch Self					Self Talk Demo Try	2 4
	Woman Entrepreneur	4				
			Survey %	2		
Power Close	Red jacket Australia	4				
					Call for Action	3
	Time Subtotal	22		8		15
				Total time = 45		

© Christine Harvey

Let's do a walk through. Notice the top line 'Main Message'. This is where you fill in either your title or simply the message you intend to deliver.

Next you'll find a block of headings. The first is 'Point'. Under this heading you'll list the points you would like to use to support your main message. Notice that I have four points to support my main message called 'You Can Do It'. My key words are 'negativity vs positivity', 'dolphin method', 'catch self', and 'power close'. The words you enter on the blank matrix that follows will be key words such as mine which remind you of your points.

The next column is headed 'Emotional Proof/Personal Incident Story'. Here you'll decide which emotional proofs you can deliver to support your point, and next to that you'll enter the time it should take to deliver that point. Notice that mine, the airplane incident, will take four minutes.

Next we look across to the following column, the 'Logical Proof/Stat/Quote/Reference'. This is where you choose a logical proof to support the *same* point. Mine is a statistic about children aged 6 to 12, which supports my point about negativity vs positivity, and it will take two minutes of my presentation.

As we look across further, we see the column 'Analogy/ Demo/Participation/Question.' This is where you draw upon your creativity by using an analogy or another of the 13 'grab and hold' methods to keep our listeners engaged. My analogy is 'pebbles in a pond', and it will take six minutes.

Creating your own fool-proof 'Matrix'

Now start thinking about your message and points. Notice that you *don't* need to restrict yourself to one proof for each point. On my second point, for example, I used three emotional proofs to support my point called 'dolphin method'. These are all key words. Dolphin method brings an entire incident to my mind, just as your key words will bring points, stories, analogies etc., to your mind.

The 'Presentation Planning Matrix' is designed to keep you on track, to give your listeners variety and to help you prove your points. It's a high impact methodology and allows you to customize your presentation or meeting content to your group. For example, if you are addressing a group of aerospace engineers, you may choose to use three of the logical/statistical type proofs for every one emotional proof. Don't be tempted, however, to eliminate the emotional/story/incident proofs and analogies. Why is that? Because stories, as we stressed before, are remembered whereas statements are forgotten. Stories have impact, statements are ignored.

Now it's time to try your hand at filling in your own matrix. In filling it in below, you'll want to review all the possible options for making your presentation powerful, with lasting impact. Regardless of whether you are giving a presentation at work, giving an after dinner speech, a wedding toast, addressing a sales conference, giving an impromptu answer to your boss, or going for a job interview, you'll want to draw upon many of these aspects of powerful communication.

Options for making your presentation powerful

- Rely upon your background, from the Monday chapter, for points and proof
- Remember to prove your point
- Give emotional proofs
- Give logical proofs
- Reiterate your point
- Don't discredit yourself
- Add powerful stories and incidents
- Use analogies
- Start the day professionally
- Use questions in your presentation
- Get audience participation
- Use demonstrations or show an object
- Use suspense or a promise
- Use humour

PRESENTATION PLANNING MATRIX							
YOUR MAIN MESSAGE _____							
Point	Emotional Proof Personal Incident Story	Time	Logical Proof Statistic/Quote/ Reference	Time	Analogy Demonstration/ Participation/ Question	Time
Time Subtotal							
Total Time =							

© *Christine Harvey*

When you are invited to speak

What if someone hears your presentation and asks you to come to speak to their group? How will you prepare for that?

I like to know the composition of the audience. How many women, how many men, how many junior and senior managers, how many salespeople, etc? This gives me a feeling of who will be listening, what level they are, what stories, emotional proof and logical proof I will use.

I also ask another question: *'When the audience leaves the room, what feeling or knowledge do you want them to be left with?'* This question lets me zero in on my main message. Then I start to connect all my points, stories, and proofs to it.

If you are starting out and speaking on a volunteer basis, you may want to simply ask a few questions over the telephone. You will want to know at least:

- The number of people expected
- Their professions
- Percentage male/female
- Their age spread
- The time allocated to you

If you start to speak on a paid basis, you may want to develop a questionnaire and ask questions such as: *'Do they want skill building?'* Or *'Do they want their people to be motivated?'* Or *'Do they want both, and in what balance?'* Other questions could be: *'Are there any sensitive issues you do not want mentioned? If so, what?'* Or, *'Are there any people or groups you want mentioned or acknowledged? If so, who?'* As you gain experience, you'll develop more questions that are important to you and your industry.

Social media application

If you intend to create video, either for incorporation in your presentation or for YouTube or for any other purpose, you'll find this chapter extremely useful. The matrix can be equally effective for a three minute message as for a 45 minute message.

With video it's essential to time your message in advance and to keep the pace fast moving for high impact. Thus a point or proof you might use in a live presentation lasting two minutes, could be cut to 20 seconds for a video. With practice you'll be able to cull the essential words to fit a 20 second segment and have it sound perfectly appropriate on video or YouTube, whereas it would sound clipped and short with a live group in a longer presentation. A promise, or one of the 13 'grab and hold' methods, is as effective here as anywhere else.

Even with Twitter, where your number of characters are so restricted, choose your words carefully to relay the highest possible impact and interest.

In preparing only written text, such as Facebook business or LinkedIn etc, you can draw upon concepts of point – proof – grab and hold, just as effectively as in your verbal presentations.

For maximum effectiveness, keep the needs of your listeners, viewers or readers in mind as you prepare your messages.

Summary

Today you were given a powerfully effective tool – The 'Presentation Planning Matrix'. This tool allows you to plot the points, and then choose options under three headings to support each. The first heading is your emotional proof relayed through a personal incident/story. The second is your logical proof relayed through statistics, quotes, and references. The third heading is that of grabbing and holding attention including analogies, demonstrations, audience participation and questions – with or without answers.

You started with your ultimate goal – the result you want to achieve. You considered whether you want your listeners to take a specific action based on your presentation, or make a specific change, or whether you simply want to relay information. Your goal will determine your main message plus the points and proofs you want to use to hammer that message home.

The matrix also allows you to consider the total time for your presentation and then break

SUNDAY MONDAY TUESDAY WEDNESDAY THURSDAY FRIDAY SATURDAY

it down into the segment times required to deliver each point, proof and analogies within your allocated time. Listeners will grasp your message and either take action or be informed, depending on your intent.

Fact-check (answers at the back)

1. In meetings, people usually don't put their points across as effectively as possible, and discussion moves on to other subjects before the matter is fully discussed. This results in
   a) decisions being made without the best ideas coming forward ❑
   b) more time for others to speak ❑
   c) the most effective use of time ❑
   d) none of the above ❑

2. Conferences rarely end on time. This is because
   a) breaks are too long ❑
   b) speakers don't time their presentations well ❑
   c) boring speakers always take longer ❑
   d) none of the above ❑

3. As a presenter, you should know how many minutes your proofs and points will take to deliver.
   a) True ❑
   b) False ❑
   c) It doesn't matter ❑
   d) None of the above ❑

4. The Presentation Planning Matrix in this chapter is designed to help you in what ways?
   a) To keep you on track ❑
   b) To give your listeners variety ❑
   c) To prove your points ❑
   d) All of the above ❑

5. When providing proofs for your points, you don't need to restrict yourself to one proof per point.
   a) True ❑
   b) False ❑
   c) It doesn't matter ❑
   d) None of the above ❑

6. It's not good to use both an emotional proof and a logical proof to support the same point.
   a) True ❑
   b) False ❑
   c) It doesn't matter ❑
   d) None of the above ❑

7. The Presentation Planning Matrix allows you to
   a) customize your presentation to your audience ❑
   b) plan the number of points you'll use in advance ❑
   c) plan the number of proofs you'll use in advance ❑
   d) all of the above ❑

8. The Matrix also allows you to
   a) have high impact with your proof ❑
   b) deliver with a high degree of professionalism ❑
   c) end on time while still including all your points effectively ❑
   d) all of the above ❑

9. If you're going to speak at a conference, a good question to ask the organizer in advance is:
   a) How long should I speak? ❏
   b) What is the composition of the audience? ❏
   c) When the audience leaves the room, what feeling or knowledge do you want them to be left with? ❏
   d) All of the above ❏

10. If you start to speak on a paid basis, you may want to
   a) ask if there are any sensitive issues they don't want mentioned ❏
   b) develop a questionnaire so that you can customize your talk to the needs of the group ❏
   c) ask if there are people or groups they want acknowledged ❏
   d) all of the above ❏

SUNDAY

MONDAY

TUESDAY

WEDNESDAY

THURSDAY

FRIDAY

SATURDAY

SATURDAY

Put icing on the cake of professionalism

Now it's time to put the icing on the cake. You've learned how to plan and deliver your presentation for high impact. But what about the extras that might come up?

For example, the way you handle questions and answers after your presentation, can help you stand above the crowd professionally. Or, how you handle a microphone – you'll want to avoid annoying feedback.

And, what about introducing guest speakers? You'll learn about a 1 – 3 – 6 – 1 formula that makes introductions a breeze. And, you'll have an equally effective guideline for thanking a speaker. And, finally there are awards, wedding toasts and even eulogies. You'll be able to give these with an air of professionalism by using the uniquely helpful formulas included here.

Thus in this chapter you will learn:

How to breeze through Q & A sessions
The pros and cons of PowerPoint presentations
How to handle a microphone
A powerful formula for introducing a guest speaker
How to prepare your own introduction
Formulas for weddings and eulogies
How to thank a speaker
How to graciously give and accept awards
Social media applications

Breeze through Q & A sessions

Your listeners love variety. They don't want just one offering. They've heard your speech. That was the main course and they've had enough. Now they want to participate. They want the surprise element. Your Q & A session is their dessert – the icing on the cake, a smorgasbord of desserts!

There's no need to fear the questions, in fact the Q & A session gives you a chance to expand on your points, and often allows you to restate the credibility of your points.

When answering, give yourself time to think. A good way to do this is to repeat the question. Listeners like this. They can't always hear the question. And while you are repeating the question, ideas will rush to your head. Trust yourself, they will.

In addition there are two methods of generating ideas as you repeat the question. One is to prepare a list of points in advance that you couldn't fit into your presentation. Glance at it as you repeat the question. Choose a point that could link to the question asked. Then start to talk about it and weave your answer in the direction of the question.

The second method is to think of your life experiences even vaguely relating to the question. Let yourself start to talk about those areas, and then more material will come to your mind related to the question as you speak. Try to review your experiences from the Monday chapter exercises before your presentation so that your mind will respond more quickly.

Always thank the questioner immediately *before* you give the answer. This makes you feel good, the questioner feel good, and the audience feel good. It sets up rapport between you and them.

Give acknowledgment

You can say one of the following:

'Thank you for that question.'

'That's an excellent question.'

'I'm glad you asked that.'

'Thank you.'

You'll find the 'thank you' that you give to the first questioner will set up a safe environment for others to ask questions. It brings harmony into the room. Don't neglect it.

The pros and cons of PowerPoint presentations

There are definite pros and cons to using PowerPoint slides during your presentation.

The negative side is this. While people are looking at the screen, what do you think they are connecting with – you or the screen? Yes, the screen, of course. Thus you may lose that all important connection.

The positive side is this. Your listeners can take in your points through their visual senses as well as their hearing senses.

If you watch the most powerful company CEOs and professional speakers, you'll notice that they seldom use PowerPoint slides at all, and if so, they use them as an accent. They may put up an important point once or twice in a 20 to 40 minute presentation.

But let's say you like PowerPoint slides or that it's expected in your industry or company. What now? How do you make it the best it can be and still connect with your listeners? The best way is to reduce the number of words. Some professionals think that six words should be the maximum per slide. And of course, pictures are worth a 1000 words. Often a good sketch and a few words make your presentation memorable.

However, as you learned in previous chapters, the picture you paint through your incident/story will have far more lasting impact than a sketch on a slide. Why? Because you create an emotional link with your story, and with your eye contact, that cannot be created between a viewer and a slide.

Remember too, that if you like visual media, there are many other options besides PowerPoint slides. You might consider video clips, clips from YouTube, or even music if the lyrics match your message and suit your audience.

It's your presentation and your group. So experiment and try to move out of the traditional box. Doing so will not only bring you satisfaction it will be a relief to your listeners to have variety and something new.

How to handle a microphone

Perhaps you'll be asked to use a microphone during your presentation. What then? Should you turn it down? If not, why not?

Look at it this way. Without a microphone, people won't hear you well and they'll be annoyed. They've come to hear you and suddenly they're at a disadvantage if you don't use it.

Secondly, you've taken time and great effort to prepare your presentation. Logically, why would you not want it to be heard? The answer is simple. It's fear. And fear comes from lack of practice. The solution is practice. You should practise now because you never know when someone will thrust a microphone into your hand and you'll have to use it. It's true. I've seen it happen to people many, many times.

If you act uncomfortably with a microphone, it will draw more attention to yourself. You probably want just the opposite. My guess is that you want high professionalism.

So let's practise now.

Practise using the microphone now

First, take a piece of ordinary paper and roll it up into a one inch diameter roll. Now hold it up on an angle of 45 degrees from your mouth.

Most neophytes hold it straight up. Don't do that. That's wrong for two reasons. First it doesn't pick up sound properly when it's straight up and down and can set off a ghastly feedback noise. It picks up better sound when facing your mouth. Secondly if you hold it up and down, it tips you off as a neophyte. Someone from the sound department might have to come to your rescue and show you how to do it in front of everyone. That's bound to distress you *and* your listeners. Better to practise it now.

Next is distance. How close, how far from the mouth? The answer is this – fist distance! Practise like this. Hold your 'paper microphone' in one hand. Now make a fist with your other hand and put it up to your lips. Then put the mic on the other side of your fist. That's the right distance. If you put it closer, the sound will really be distorted. Again the system can give off feedback and hurt everyone's ears. If you put it further away, it doesn't pick up your sound.

Lapel or earpiece microphone

Of course if you have a lapel or ear piece mic, and *if* the sound people wire you up and check it in advance, you don't have too much to worry about. Just be sure you don't bang it as you move, and always remember to turn it off at breaks during personal discussions or use of the ladies'/men's rooms. Don't laugh. It happens often!

SUNDAY
MONDAY
TUESDAY
WEDNESDAY
THURSDAY
FRIDAY
SATURDAY

Powerful formula for introducing a guest speaker

If you've ever had to introduce a speaker, did you consider it a privilege and opportunity that you looked forward to with joy? Or did you anticipate it with shaky knees?

If you are like most people, it was the latter. There are probably two reasons.

1 Lack of professional 'know how' and practice.
2 Not being sure what to say.

In this section you will conquer both roadblocks. Consider this. You have the privilege of setting the meeting tone and mood. You can make it wonderful. You can make the audience feel privileged. You can make the topic important. You can make the speaker important – and indeed they are, or you would not have invited them to address your group.

Look at it this way. If the speaker talks for 45 minutes, and you have 20 people attending, that's 15 man hours being used to listen to that speaker. The same 15 man hours could be used for something else, but they are not. People are there to hear your speaker. Isn't it worth giving them an introduction that sets a positive tone? Of course it is. If you don't, the audience will wish they hadn't come. So set aside your anxieties and dig into the most professional introduction you can create.

Here is a superb introduction formula from our Effective Presentation Seminars. It's professional and gives credit where credit is due. It makes your attendees happy they've come, and it puts you in a good light.

The 1-3-6-1 formula for introductions

A. Subject or Title – Give **1** sentence

B. Why important to group – Give **3** examples

C. Why speaker is qualified – Give **6** reasons

D. Welcome speaker – Give **1** name

> When you flesh it out it will sound like this:
>
> **A.** The subject (or title of our talk) today is ...
>
> **B.** The subject is important to us because ... (give 3 reasons)
>
> **C.** Our speaker is extremely qualified because ...
> (give 6 qualifications)
>
> **D.** Please help me welcome ... (Name)

Preparing your own introduction

When I first started speaking professionally, I read that speakers should prepare their own introduction. I was quite shocked by this idea. It seemed very arrogant.

The writer went on to say that we are the professionals and it is important to the audience to find out who is speaking to them and why they are qualified. He warned that it is foolhardy not to prepare our own introduction, because without it, the organizers won't know what to say. It is our *obligation* to brief them, for the sake of the audience.

Since then, I've discovered this advice to be sound. I've discovered that the majority of conference organizers welcome introductions prepared by speakers. It takes the worry out of it for them. Why? Because they know that you will be happy with it, that it's accurate and it's professionally prepared. It makes them look good too.

Simply follow the 1-3-6-1 formula for preparing your own introduction.

On the few occasions in which the introduction didn't reach the correct person before the speech, I've found that one of three things can happen. All are detrimental.

First is that the facts are often wrong because the introducer was not briefed properly. The second is that the introducer, often ill at ease with speaking, tries to make a joke as part of the introduction and it fails miserably. Third is that they fail to set up the importance of your speech topic to the audience. This failure to link your topic to the audience's interests or needs, gives your speech a not-so-promising start.

What steps should you take therefore in briefing your introducer? Simply email or fax an introduction which is specifically prepared for each group. Include a cover letter, saying that they may use it in full or in part. Thus you've taken a load off their shoulders and given them permission to shorten it if they wish.

Let's move on to other uses for the 1-3-6-1 formula.

Formula for wedding speeches and toasts

The 1-3-6-1 formula can be used for wedding speeches as well. It looks like this.

A Give 1 sentence about the reason you are all there ... (To honour the bride and groom and families, etc.)

B Give 3 memories you have of the groom and/or bride and why they are important in your life. An incident/story is powerful here.

C Give 6 wishes you have for their future ... (blessings for their health, happiness, prosperity, etc.)

D Propose your toast.

Formula for eulogies

Eulogies follow the same format except that point C should include six of the person's qualities and/or achievements in life and career, as well as their impact on family, friends, community, etc. Point D can be a prayer or a wish from your heart.

Now let's move on to thanking a guest speaker or conference speaker.

How to thank a speaker

If you've been chosen to thank a speaker, start by considering it to be an honour, just as we discussed in introducing a speaker. Here too you have an opportunity to uplift your event, making both the audience and speaker feel honoured. That's important for the morale of the group.

With the formula below, you will *not* have to worry ahead of time. You will use this as a framework and fill in the appropriate points *as the speaker speaks*.

In fact, it's far better not to prepare a thank you in advance because it will not link closely to the speaker's message. This 'canned' approach can be interpreted as superficial to the audience and speaker. It's better to use the formula below and speak from your heart, unless of course you have the speaker's text in advance.

Formula for thanking a speaker

You'll be surprised how easily this formula can be used on the spot.

1 **Thank you**, (Name)
2 **What the person said** that: *(choose one)*

   a) you liked

   b) helped you, or

   c) caught your attention

3 **Group benefit**: What the person said that is likely to help or benefit the group.

4 **How you'll remember** the speaker and their contribution (For example, 'Every time I see a rose in the future, I know I'll think of your helpful suggestions about horticulture.'
5 **Express appreciation** for their time and sharing their expertise. If you are presenting a gift, do that now.
6 **Thank**: Please join me in thanking, (Name of speaker) Start the applause.

Give and accept awards

Now let's look at another aspect of speaking, that of giving and receiving awards. Even if you're not going to give or receive an award now, it will prepare you in developing your professionalism. And who knows – you may receive an award when you least expect it!

Present an award

In giving awards, it's quite suspenseful if you leave the name of the award winner until the end, just as we did in the introduction.

Formula for presenting an award

1 **What** the award is and why the award was created.
2 **Who** chose the winner.
3 **Why** that winner was chosen.
4 **Who** won (Name) Then, applaud.
5 Invite the winner to the front, present the award or plaque, shake hands, and applaud again.

Let's look at an example. It's one we use in our seminars to acknowledge one person who shows exceptional promise:

Example

1 *'It's my pleasure to present to one of you this gold plated pen, with this inscription.* (Hold the pen up and read the inscription.) *This award was created to acknowledge exceptional contribution.*

2 *You, the winner, were chosen by the vote of your fellow delegates.*
3 *You were chosen on the basis of the action plans you devised, which you will carry out when you get back to the office.*
4 *Now, it's with great pleasure that I present this award, on behalf of your fellow delegates to* (Name).'
(Applaud)
5 *'Please come to the front.'* (Shake hands and give award).
(Applaud)

How to accept an award

If you are going to accept an award sometime in the future, memorize this simple format. It will be easy to follow as you stand and accept the award. It will be sincere and spontaneous and the group will love your response.

Formula for accepting an award

1 **Thank** those responsible.
2 Tell what the **award means** to you.
3 Tell how you'll **use the award**, or where you'll display it.
4 Tell how you'll **remember the group** fondly.
5 **Thank** them again.

Example

1 *'I want to thank all of you, my fellow delegates, for voting for me. I'm highly honoured. I also want to thank Mrs Leventhal and Mr Brown, our instructors, for their support.*
2 *This award means a lot to me and I commit to you now to put everything into practice as we discussed in this workshop.*
3 *I'm going to keep this pen close to my heart here (shows breast pocket of jacket) and*
4 *Every time I use it, I'll think of our group and your support.*
5 *Thank you very much.'*

When you sit down after your acceptance talk, you'll feel very good about yourself. That's important. Don't give in to a simple *'Thank you'* or worse yet, the humble denial, *'I hardly deserve this... .'* Why? Because these discredit those who chose you. You are a winner. Otherwise you wouldn't be chosen. By visualizing yourself accepting an award calmly and composed, you'll handle it as an everyday event when the time comes.

Have you ever watched people presenting and accepting awards in the film industry on television? If so, you'll notice that the same fundamentals are followed. We discover who gave the award and why. The winner thanks those responsible and says why they appreciate the award.

If your award presentation is going to be televised or filmed on video, you should practise the eye contact exercises in Sunday's chapter. Don't let yourself be distracted by the lights or the cameras. Ignore them and keep concentrating on the audience. If you act naturally, you'll come across as a professional. If you do need to look directly into the camera, which happens in some interviews, keep concentrating on the fact that there is only one person sitting in their own living room watching you. Think of it like a conversation, and you'll be fine.

Social media application

Let's think about all the points covered in this chapter as they could relate to the various social media outlets. As we said in the beginning, the points in this chapter are the icing on the cake of professionalism.

On YouTube and any use of video, how you handle the microphone is paramount. You won't want to make the mistake of some YouTube presenters who have a stationary mic positioned on their desk, and then proceed to shift their body back and forth away from the mic. This results in the sound level going from high to low, high to low, and high to low, like a yoyo! If you like to move around a lot, then a lapel or an earpiece mic is the best solution. Some presenters like the look and feel of a hand-held mic, or a stationary mic on a table top is fine, but then you must keep your mouth the same distance from the mic at all times, even if you move your hands and arms for emphasis.

What about virtual meetings, teleconferences and web conferencing? There you'll have an opportunity to introduce and thank guest speakers according to the formulas in this chapter.

With teleconferences and video you may find a PowerPoint format to be effective, utilizing a few key words rather than long sentences or jam-packed slides.

Q & A can be effectively utilized in both video/YouTube and text formats, even if you are the sole presenter. Simply use the most common or relevant questions, attributing them to a person if appropriate, and then give your answer.

Be sure to refer to the social media sections near the end of each chapter to maximize your personal impact.

A final word

In closing, I'd like to thank you all for reading this book and preparing to heighten your communication, personal impact and leadership skills. Dale Carnegie, the legendary instructor of public speaking, was once told that the graduates from his course were more powerful speakers than most senators in the United States. This will happen to you as you apply these principles. As I said in the introduction, it's a pity to have a good education but not be able to put a point across with high impact. That's not something we're born with, it's something we must learn and practise.

I'm often asked how to continue advancement of these skills. In addition to our courses on Personal Impact, you might want to try the Dale Carnegie Human Relations course, which is run worldwide, or join a local Toastmasters Club, also worldwide. All three are different, and all are extremely effective. For further information on this or any aspect of the book, feel free to contact me by email at ChristineHarvey@ChrisitneHarvey.com or via the publishers.

Now go forward and let your thoughts be known! Your ideas are important to the world.

Christine Harvey

Summary

Today you learned that listeners love variety and that Q & A sessions are like a smorgasbord of desserts for them. You learned to repeat their question, thus giving your mind time to conceive your answer. You also learned two ways to jog your mind for answers, including a pre-prepared bullet list and reliance on your background strengths.

You learned several high impact formulas to use for specific presentations. These include the 1-3-6-1 formula for introducing a speaker, preparing your own introduction, wedding and eulogy speeches, plus thanking a speaker, and presenting and accepting an award. All of these formulas provide you with a fool-proof way to make your job easy and your professionalism high.

And what if you choose to use PowerPoint slides? You discovered that they can disconnect you from your audience, and that limited use is best, especially with limited number of words per screen. Additionally you had practice using a microphone. Yes, practice, even without the mic! You learned that the 'fist' distance and the 45 degree angle of the mic are all important in avoiding the screeching sound of mic feedback.

Fact-check (answers at the back)

1. There is no need to fear Q & A sessions because they give you the following benefits:
   a) A chance to expand on your points ☐
   b) A chance to restate your credibility, giving validity to your points ☐
   c) None of the above ☐
   d) All of the above ☐

2. In Q & A sessions it's a good idea to repeat the question before you answer because
   a) it gives you time to think ☐
   b) it allows listeners to hear the question well ☐
   c) while you repeat it, answers will come to your mind ☐
   d) all of the above ☐

3. There are two good methods for generating your answers during Q & A. They are:
   a) Refer to a pre-prepared bullet list ☐
   b) Think back over your wide ranging experience ☐
   c) Both of the above ☐
   d) None of the above ☐

4. During Q & A it's always good to thank the person asking the question. Why?
   a) It makes you feel good ☐
   b) It makes the questioner feel good ☐
   c) It makes the audience feel good ☐
   d) All of the above ☐

5. Why do PowerPoint slides often cause you to lose connection with your audience?
   a) You lose eye contact ☐
   b) You lose emotional link ☐
   c) Both of the above ☐
   d) Neither of the above ☐

6. When using microphones, the two most important factors are angle and distance. How far should the mic be from your lips?
   a) two inches ☐
   b) finger distance ☐
   c) fist distance ☐
   d) six inches ☐

7. The introduction formula is called 1 – 3 – 6 – 1. What does the 3 stand for?
   a) 3 minutes before the presentation starts ☐
   b) 3 reasons the message will be important to the group ☐
   c) 3 questions that must be answered ☐
   d) 3 people who would be involved ☐

8. It's okay to prepare your own introduction and pass it on to the conference organizer because
   a) it sets up the right background for your presentation ☐
   b) it takes a load off the organizer ☐
   c) both a and b above ☐
   d) neither a nor b above ☐

9. In thanking a speaker, it is better to
a) prepare your comments in advance ☐
b) prepare your comments as they speak, using the formula ☐
c) pass the job on to someone else ☐
d) none of the above ☐

10. In accepting an award, it's a good idea to
a) thank those responsible ☐
b) tell what the award means to you ☐
c) tell how you'll use or display the award ☐
d) all of the above ☐

Surviving in tough times

Whether you are an employee, a manager or a business owner, tough times present enormous challenges. You've probably never been stretched to use your full potential as much as you are in tough times. No doubt you've had to step out of your comfort zone for job interviews or major management decisions or hiring and firing.

Regardless of the challenges, you will be well served if you focus on the principles of 'personal impact'. For example, you'll need to prove your point effectively with customers, colleagues and shareholders. You'll need to lend credibility to yourself and your company. You'll need to structure your presentations to make your message stick.

Here are ten 'personal impact' tips you can implement quickly for great results.

1 Use credibility prefaces

From now on when you speak, use credibility prefaces from the Monday chapter. For example, instead of saying, 'Let's try XYZ' say this: 'When I headed up the special committee for ABC, we discovered that the XYZ method worked best. I'm sure we can get the same high results here. Let's try it.' By using a credibility preface you are giving your listeners faith in you and in your suggestion. This will lead to promotions, new job offers, support from your staff and often to higher income in your career or business.

2 Take the most challenging path

I once gave a talk titled, 'When you come to a crossroad in life, take the most challenging path'. Six months later an attendee told me this: 'After your presentation I applied the principle to everything at work – meetings, phone calls, email. I asked myself: "What's the most challenging path?" and then I did it.' Consequently he had two promotions, increases in pay, and his confidence was at an all time high.

I urge you to do the same. Many of the principles in these chapters will force you to take the challenging path. Yet, like this man, the sky is the limit when you commit to employing them.

3 Everyone lives by selling something

Perhaps you've never thought of yourself as needing to sell anything, yet we all need to sell our ideas. Practise making your point clearly and then supporting it with logical and emotional proofs. These will include statistics, quotes, numbers, and references, as well as stories/incidents that touch the emotion of your listeners. Both types of proofs are necessary when selling your ideas. Whether it's convincing our spouse, our kids, our boss or our staff, we are selling ideas. Whether you're pitching for a promotion, a new job or motivating your staff for higher performance, take heed of the points in the Tuesday chapter.

4 Motivate your staff and colleagues

Many bosses think that pay is the top motivator. Yet ranking higher is recognition for a job well done. If you want to motivate your staff for higher performance and loyalty in tough times, refer to the awards section in the Saturday chapter. Awards cost practically nothing to create and have high impact.

It's not the monetary value of the award that counts. Instead it's being recognized in front of their peers for the time, effort and talent they have contributed. Awards such as plaques, framed certificates and engraved pens can be created immediately. They also set an example and encourage others to strive for their best performance.

5 Raise your exposure

In my book, *In Pursuit of Profit*, I point out that the people who get ahead fastest are the ones who can put their ideas across most effectively. This gives people exposure. In tough times, you need exposure for new business opportunities and promotions. Take a moment to reflect. Which of the principles in this book will lead to better exposure for you? Consider credibility prefaces from the Monday chapter and putting power in your presentations in the remaining chapters. Then master them one by one.

6 Ditch the comfort zone

Moving out of your comfort zone is never easy, yet it's essential. In another of my books, *Secrets of the World's Top Sales Performers*, a high flyer advised, *'When trying something new, tell yourself "you can do it, you can do it."'* Go out on a limb and *DO* it – perfect your personal impact. Learn to prove your point in the Tuesday and Wednesday chapters. Use proofs of your ability, and stories or statistics to prove your points. Use it with the boss, in meetings, in presentations, in job interviews and for promotions.

7 Put your point across powerfully

You've spent years in education and probably years in job training. Isn't it time for you to build the greatest expertise you possibly can in putting yourself and your point of view across to the maximum? By doing so, you'll be seen as a powerful leader. Think of all the ways you'll be able to apply your newfound expertise – one to one with your boss, colleagues, people in the community, as well as in presentations. And the best part is this. It won't take you as long as your education took you, and yet the results – both in monetary and satisfaction terms will be great. Start with the non-verbal actions in the Sunday chapter and move forward.

8 Pitch for promotion

If you're pitching for a promotion, use the matrix in the Friday chapter to plot out the points leading to your promotion message. For example, '*I am the best qualified person for the promotion.*' Then list your proofs based on your past performance and your abilities. And don't forget your 'call for action' close, actually asking for a positive decision. And finally, don't forget to draw upon the Monday chapter principle of 'credibility prefaces' for your points. These are indeed essential for high impact.

9 Stay on course

Use the 13 'grab and hold' attention techniques from the Thursday chapter anytime a meeting goes off course. Bring it back on course. Perhaps higher productivity or increasing the customer base or whatever is needed by your company. This puts you in a good light and helps the company as well.

10 Leadership is in demand

Leadership is in *big* demand. Few people are seen as capable. Being technically good is no longer enough. Show that you have leadership skills by practising the principles in the Saturday chapter. Step up to answer difficult customer questions, and use the 1-3-6-1 formula to introduce guests at any formal presentation. Use the principles of the Tuesday chapter to prove your points masterfully in every possible setting. Master the presentation planning techniques in the Friday chapter. Complete and expand on your impact journal as you study the material, and it will become a truly valuable resource for you.

Answers

Sunday: 1d; 2c; 3b; 4c; 5a; 6d; 7b;
8d; 9d; 10a

Monday: 1b; 2d; 3d; 4d; 5d; 6d;
7a; 8d; 9d; 10b

Tuesday: 1c; 2c; 3c; 4a; 5b; 6c;
7a; 8d; 9c; 10c

Wednesday: 1d; 2d; 3d; 4c; 5d;
6d; 7d; 8b; 9d; 10d

Thursday: 1a; 2a; 3d; 4b; 5d; 6d;
7d; 8a; 9d; 10d

Friday: 1a; 2b; 3a; 4d; 5a; 6b; 7d;
8d; 9d; 10d

Saturday: 1d; 2d; 3c; 4d; 5c; 6c;
7b; 8c; 9b; 10d

Notes

ALSO AVAILABLE IN THE 'IN A WEEK' SERIES

BODY LANGUAGE FOR MANAGEMENT ● BOOKKEEPING AND ACCOUNTING ● CUSTOMER CARE ● SPEED READING ● DEALING WITH DIFFICULT PEOPLE ● EMOTIONAL INTELLIGENCE ● FINANCE FOR NON-FINANCIAL MANAGERS ● INTRODUCING MANAGEMENT ● MANAGING YOUR BOSS ● MARKET RESEARCH ● NEURO-LINGUISTIC PROGRAMMING ● OUTSTANDING CREATIVITY ● PLANNING YOUR CAREER ● SUCCEEDING AT INTERVIEWS ● SUCCESSFUL APPRAISALS ● SUCCESSFUL ASSERTIVENESS ● SUCCESSFUL BUSINESS PLANS ● SUCCESSFUL CHANGE MANAGEMENT ● SUCCESSFUL COACHING ● SUCCESSFUL COPYWRITING ● SUCCESSFUL CVS ● SUCCESSFUL INTERVIEWING

For information about other titles in the series, please visit www.inaweek.co.uk

ALSO AVAILABLE IN THE 'IN A WEEK' SERIES

SUCCESSFUL JOB APPLICATIONS • SUCCESSFUL JOB HUNTING
• SUCCESSFUL KEY ACCOUNT MANAGEMENT • SUCCESSFUL LEADERSHIP
• SUCCESSFUL MARKETING • SUCCESSFUL MARKETING PLANS
• SUCCESSFUL MEETINGS • SUCCESSFUL MEMORY TECHNIQUES
• SUCCESSFUL MENTORING • SUCCESSFUL NEGOTIATING • SUCCESSFUL
NETWORKING • SUCCESSFUL PEOPLE SKILLS • SUCCESSFUL
PRESENTING • SUCCESSFUL PROJECT MANAGEMENT • SUCCESSFUL
PSYCHOMETRIC TESTING • SUCCESSFUL PUBLIC RELATIONS •
SUCCESSFUL RECRUITMENT • SUCCESSFUL SELLING • SUCCESSFUL
STRATEGY • SUCCESSFUL TIME MANAGEMENT • TACKLING INTERVIEW
QUESTIONS

For information about other titles
in the series, please visit
www.inaweek.co.uk

LEARN IN A WEEK,
WHAT THE EXPERTS
LEARN IN A LIFETIME

For information about other titles
in the series, please visit
www.inaweek.co.uk